Edward Albee

MICHIGAN MODERN DRAMATISTS
Enoch Brater, Series Editor

Michigan Modern Dramatists offers the theatergoer concise, accessible, and indispensable guides to the works of individual playwrights, as interpreted by today's leading drama critics.

Edward Albee

Toby Zinman

THE UNIVERSITY OF MICHIGAN PRESS

ANN ARBOR

Copyright © by the University of Michigan 2008
All rights reserved
Published in the United States of America by
The University of Michigan Press
Manufactured in the United States of America
◎ Printed on acid-free paper

2011   2010   2009   2008   4   3   2   1

A CIP catalog record for this book is available from the British Library.

Library of Congress Cataloging-in-Publication Data

Zinman, Toby Silverman, 1942–
     Edward Albee / Toby Zinman.
        p.   cm. — (Michigan modern dramatists)
     Includes bibliographical references.
     ISBN-13: 978-0-472-09919-1 (cloth : acid-free paper)
     ISBN-10: 0-472-09919-1 (cloth : acid-free paper)
     ISBN-13: 978-0-472-06919-4 (pbk. : acid-free paper)
     ISBN-10: 0-472-06919-5 (pbk. : acid-free paper)
        1. Albee, Edward, 1928—Criticism and interpretation.   2. Albee,
     Edward, 1928—Bibliography.   3. Albee, Edward, 1928—Stories,
     plots, etc.   I. Title.

PS3551.L25Z96   2008
812'.54—dc22   2007035402

For Ph, L&K, YM

Acknowledgments

It gives me pleasure to thank: Enoch Brater and LeAnn Fields for their editorial encouragement; the University of the Arts for a grant and the Institute for U.S. Studies at the University of London for a visiting fellowship that allowed me to pursue this work during the summer of 2004; Jakob Holder at the Albee Foundation; and Jo Ann McDowell and Dawson Moore at the Last Frontier Playwrights Conference.

I am especially grateful to my undergraduate students at the University of the Arts when we spent a semester together in the spring of 2004 working on Albee's plays; their enthusiasm and insights inform much of this book.

And, of course, many thanks to Edward Albee, for the plays.

A Note on Sources

All quotations not otherwise attributed come from Albee's *Collected Plays* in three volumes (Woodstock, NY: Overlook Duckworth, 2004–5), cited by volume number and page. References to Albee's *Stretching My Mind* (New York: Caroll and Graf, 2005) are abbreviated *SMM*; Mel Gussow's biography *Edward Albee: A Singular Journey* (New York: Applause, 2001) is cited as *ASJ*. Other sources are listed in the bibliography.

Contents

1   Introduction

10   *Peter and Jerry: "Homelife"* and *The Zoo Story*

16   *The Zoo Story*

21   *The Death of Bessie Smith*

29   *The Sandbox*

35   *The American Dream*

39   *Who's Afraid of Virginia Woolf?*

53   *Tiny Alice*

62   *A Delicate Balance*

69   *Box* and *Quotations from Chairman Mao Tse-Tung*

74   *All Over*

79   *Seascape*

87   *Listening*

91   *Counting the Ways: A Vaudeville*

99   *The Lady from Dubuque*

103   *The Man Who Had Three Arms*

107   *Finding the Sun*

112   *Marriage Play*

118   *Three Tall Women*

125   *Fragments*

132   *The Play About the Baby*

139   *The Goat or, Who Is Sylvia?*

151   *Occupant*

156   *Knock! Knock! Who's There!?*

159   Bibliography

161   Chronology of Plays

Introduction

Edward Albee's career began with a shocking play, shocking in both its content and its redefinition of realism; *The Zoo Story* would radically alter American theater in the second half of the twentieth century. And it is splendid that nearly half a century later, *The Goat* shocked American audiences and critics again.

Albee's prolific career, studded with three Pulitzer Prizes and the prestigious Tony Award for Lifetime Achievement, is still in full swing. His newest play, an as yet unpublished "prequel" to *The Zoo Story*, is called "Homelife" and opened on May 20, 2004; Albee is currently working on several scripts including one called "Me, Myself and I" about a doppelgänger (sounds more like a tripleganger to me). His plays have been seen in major revival after major revival, on and off Broadway, in recent seasons. Albee's drama over the years has been both praised and reviled, but he has remained an immense force on the contemporary stage, reshaping the theatrical mainstream while remaining outside it. His plays are populated by literate, articulate, witty, self-aware characters whose civilized lives are shredded by powerful forces; those forces are both internal and external, both personal and metaphysical; the flashpoint is the intersection where the mythic meets the pedestrian. Many of his characters make the fundamental human discovery that they have tried bravely and failed miserably, but that there was nothing, finally, to be done, life being what it is, they being who they are.

With the recent publication of *The Collected Plays of Edward Albee* in three volumes, the structure of this book became obvious: I have written about each play, following the chronological order through volume 1 (1958–65), volume 2 (1966–77), and volume 3 (1978–2003), reflecting forward and backward as the needs arise. That said, I have begun by violating chronological order, by starting with "Homelife"; although this is Albee's latest play, he wrote it as a first act to his first play, *The Zoo Story*, and dramatic sense rather than strict chronology ruled; thus the earliest and the latest plays launch this discussion. Each of the plays has its own essay, facilitating access for the reader who, having seen a production or read a script, wants to know more. I imagine these essays as the basis of a silent dialogue between us ("So, what did you think?"), attempting to provide insight into Albee's concerns and techniques as well as links to the biography, to other plays, and to other playwrights. The only works omitted from discussion are Albee's adaptations from other authors *(The Ballad of the Sad Café, Malcolm, Everything in the Garden,* and *Lolita).* These rarely performed plays raise issues that would consume too much space: the pros and cons of contravening genre-specificity, the fundamental differences between fiction and drama, as well as my interpretation of each original work versus my interpretation of Albee's (which in the case of Nabokov would require immense analysis).

Although each of the following essays addresses Albee's themes as they emerge from a particular play, this introduction provides an overview of his recurrent preoccupations, motions of mind traceable over nearly half a century . The strategy here is to allow the reader to see how links between and among Albee's plays can be reconfigured; this roaming through the canon can be a rich experience, providing readers with the wherewithal to come to their own understandings and appreciations, rather than merely react to hermetically sealed interpretations. My reluctance to promote a particular way of reading a play (or all the plays), that is, holding up a feminist or Marxist or Freudian lens through which to read or watch, echoes Albee's firm views. In "Read Plays?" Albee insists that reading scripts is as rewarding as seeing productions, where the playwright's work may have been altered by the actors and the director: "I'm not suggesting you should not see plays. There are a lot of swell productions, but keep in mind a production is an opinion, an interpretation. . . . Of course, *your* reading of a play is *also* an opinion, an interpretation, but there are fewer hands (and minds) in the way of your engagement with the author" (257).

But he acknowledges that a playwright can interfere: "There is a tricky and magical moment: the first rehearsal. Then the playwright should go away for two and a half weeks—after it's gone to hell and begun to come back." He adds, "I suspect I've been directing my own work and others' (like Beckett's) to learn about the craft of directing so I could work intelligently with other directors and actors. My *Zoo Story* was the worst production I've ever seen. [Alan] Schneider, [Peter] Hall and [Louis] Barrault were my faculty for learning directing." Finally, he opines, "Directing is one of the most boring professions imaginable" (Playwrights Panel, June 2002, Last Frontier Theatre Conference, Valdez, Alaska).

Albee's encouragement of young writing talent is famous. Among many other efforts is his support of the Last Frontier Theatre Conference, which for thirteen years brought about four hundred people each June to the tiny town of Valdez, Alaska. In 2002, I was invited to attend as a judge, so I was able to observe Albee in action: he provided formal and informal lectures and master classes, and sat through readings of fourteen full-length plays. When he had a comment, he would modestly raise his hand, providing insights of great value. Just as his generosity toward new playwrights is legendary, so is his mistrust of actors; he told the assembly of playwrights: "Actors are not stupid. Actors are shrewd and bright, except the ones who are stupid. A sufficient minority of actors are talented, and casting is probably 95 percent of the problem solved." He went on, softening his remark, "Out of twenty-seven plays with about 250 characters, of all the hundreds of actors I've worked with, there are only four I would never work with again." In an interview in *American Theatre*, speaking about *Three Tall Women*, he said, "I always tell actors, whenever I direct, 'You can do anything you want, as long as you end up with exactly what *I* want'" ("Yes Is Better Than No," 38). With a very straight face, Albee gave this advice to a roomful of aspiring playwrights: "Be very careful about casting an actor you're sharing a bed with; either the script or the relationship will suffer." Albee mistrusts designers, too: "Be very leery of a set that wants to tell you what the play is about—a set is a container. It is impossible *not* to have a set—even a total absence of a set is a set. The only requirement is that it be right for the production; there are many possibilities for a play, as long as the designer understands the play" (Albee speaking in Valdez, Alaska, June 2002).

"Film hates words. Theater loves words."

Albee's remark in a televised interview is, like so many of his remarks, both pithy and combative, a provocation to thought. But, generally speaking, his distinction is a shrewd and incisive one, and it is certainly the case that Albee's theater loves words. He relishes definitions, puns, grammar—all part of the arsenal his articulate characters use to protect themselves, assert themselves, and attack each other. He makes considerable linguistic demands on his audiences, assuming we will rise to the occasion he provides. Language is not only the way we communicate with each other and with ourselves, it is also the one necessity to a theatrical script, the way the playwright communicates with us.

One of Albee's techniques for linguistic enjoyment is to seize on a word and candle it, hold it up to the light to see what inspection will yield. In *Counting the Ways*, for example, a character called He wonders, "Can less encroach?" (2:533). Or in *Listening*, the Man says to the Woman, "Well, you never *know*. You know?" (2:486). My favorite example is an early one from *Who's Afraid of Virginia Woolf?*: Martha, flirting with Nick, who is a biologist and not, as Martha had thought, a mathematician, says, "Good for him. Biology's even better. It's less . . . abstruse." George corrects her: "Abstract." Martha replies, "ABSTRUSE. In the sense of recondite. *(Sticks her tongue out at GEORGE)* Don't you tell me words" (1:196). Albee's plays, filled with marital battles and détentes, are always fought on a linguistic field.

Consider, for example, some of his titles: *Marriage Play* is carefully not called *The Marriage Play*, suggesting that "play" means games as well as script. The title of a later work, *The Play About the Baby*, sounds like a reference to *Who's Afraid of Virginia Woolf?* by someone who has forgotten its title and is simply describing "the play about the baby." Of course the title *is* a summary of the newer play, too, descriptive of the plot as well as suggesting the definition of "play" as it describes the cruel game about the baby that is, in fact, the plot of *The Play About the Baby*. Both *Marriage Play* and *The Play About the Baby* are filled with linguistic sparring and assaults; most of them in *Baby* are based on intimidation (Man and Woman can talk rings around Boy and Girl), while the husband and wife in *Marriage Play* are evenly matched. During what may—or may not—be the final and defining argument of their marriage, they argue over parts of speech and imperfectly remembered quotations, and Gillian tells Jack, "Oh, what a wangled teb we weave," a line later echoed by Woman in *Baby*. Practicing deception (to follow the implication of the allusion to Sir Walter Scott's "Oh, what a tangled web we weave / When first we practice to deceive") is fundamental to marriage, to communication, and to the function of language itself. Perhaps the most shocking linguistic moments come when the couple in *The Goat* have their tragic showdown; it is as if Medea and Jason, or Clytemnestra and Agamemnon, had paused to note the wit of each other's riposte.

"The manner of a play is determined by its matter"

Albee's plays vary widely in "manner"; some are short, some are long; some turn on violent action, while some are physically static; some hew to the requirements of realism, while some violate the convention of the fourth wall (that invisible wall which would hide the stage from the audience's view) and others do not. His plays are almost always tragicomic, which is to say Albee can convey the grimmest vision of life while amusing us; here lies his greatest debt to Samuel Beckett, an author he admires greatly. When asked in a public forum in Valdez if Beckett had influenced him, he replied, "We learn from our betters."

Albee's creative method, as he has described it, is to let a play incubate in his mind, without notes. Eventually, "He will test it: he will . . . introduce his characters to a situation that is not part of the play. If they behave easily and naturally—if he is able to improvise dialogue for them without effort—then he will decide that he and they know each other well enough, and he will start to write. Once he has started writing, he will write one draft, read it over, make corrections, and write out a second. Then he is finished" (MacFarquhar, 77).

Albee experiments frequently with a technique often referred to as "direct address," a character speaking directly to the audience; he returns to this technique often, from the very early *Sandbox*, where Grandma speaks to us unheard by the other characters, to the very recent *Occupant*, where the entire play is addressed to the audience from a podium. This choice (most often seen in the work of the contemporary Irish playwrights) suggests the need to violate the theatrical illusion, all the while sustaining it (a high-wire act perfected by Renaissance soliloquies). In fact, very few of his plays conform to the rules of naturalistic theater. A comment on Jonathan Thomas's paintings (Thomas was Albee's life partner from 1971 until Thomas's death in 2005) seems to comment on the effect of Albee's plays as well: "It is this vibration—this cross-fade—between the explicit and the implicit, between the totality and the construction, which gives these painting their disturbing magic" (*SMM*, 157).

"Maybe I'm a European playwright and I don't know it"

In an article about his trip to Easter Island, the fulfillment of a long-time dream, Albee wrote, "Way before the movie *Planet of the Apes* showed us the Statue of Liberty half buried in the sand, I have felt the need to experience cultures which grew, fell into decadence and vanished. These are probably cautionary tales even beyond their aesthetic marvel" ("Easter Island," 1). Albee's affinity for "cautionary tales" is clear in many of his plays, and it is in this widest sense that they may be called political, and thus may be called European.

American drama is generally preoccupied with the psychology of dysfunctional families; the focus is usually on battling brothers who are still competing for parental love or attention or money; these brothers are already grown men, and thus their sibling rivalry can be seen as protracted adolescence. Benedict Nightingale called this "diaper drama" and Martin Esslin addresses it in "'Dead! And Never Called Me Mother!'" Consider this brief list of major American plays that reflect this same parent-child dynamic: Eugene O'Neill's *Long Day's Journey Into Night*, Arthur Miller's *Death of a Salesman*, Tennessee Williams's *Cat on a Hot Tin Roof*, Sam Shepard's *True West*, and Suzan-Lori Parks's *Top Dog/Underdog*. This may well be a reflection of a nation self-defined by a psychological civil war, as well as the Civil War and its lingering, unresolved brother-against-brother issues. Unlike these other major American playwrights, Albee's preoccupation is with adult relationships, particularly upper-middle-class marriage. The internecine battles between husbands and wives may be seen as a reflection of American society in tormented collapse, the shredding of the fabric of hope, the betrayal of the values of that social institution which emblematizes the joining of like-minded people and a commitment to the future. This focus on mature relationships and, by extension, the focus on self-understanding, is far more philosophic than psychologic, and is more frequently a characteristic of British and European drama than of American drama.

The famous line from *Who's Afraid of Virginia Woolf?*, "Truth and illusion. Who knows the difference, eh, toots?" illuminates Albee's views about life as well as relationships—relationship to oneself as well as to others. Of course, theatrical art, dependent as it is on both truth and illusion, is at the heart of the matter. His characters often consciously playact or create plays within plays, delivering lines, striking poses. Most significant are the offspring of these toxic marriages—usually one son (sometimes imaginary)—who either vanishes, or dies, or is mute or betrayed or stolen. The heart-wrenching conceit of the illusory child comes and goes throughout the plays; consider all the ambiguous children who haunt the Albee canon, including those in *American Dream*, *Who's Afraid of Virginia Woolf?*, *A Delicate Balance*, *Three Tall Women*, *Listening*, *The Play About the Baby*, *Finding the Sun*, and *The Goat*.

"And what is gained is loss"

In this succinct line from *The Zoo Story*, Albee expressed his vision of life in his first play—and, tellingly, expressed it through wordplay.

This idea would sustain many—perhaps all—of his plays in the five decades following *The Zoo Story*. He has modulated this grim idea of inevitable loss (of love, of innocence, of expectation) into a deeply ironical meditation on life, reminiscent of Jaques in Shakespeare's *As You Like It*; one loses not only teeth, hair, eyes, but, finally, "everything." When an interviewer asked if he found it ironic that *Three Tall Women* was acclaimed as a "new play" when it was already several years old, Albee replied, "There's irony for me in everything" ("Yes Is Better Than No," 38).

The inevitable loss, regardless of the encroachments of bifocals and receding hairline, is of mortal time. Albee's constant subject is time's pressures and its passage; sometimes this is revealed paradoxically, as in *All Over* when the play's leisurely pace is held in tension with the last hour of the dying man's life, or in *Seascape*, where the very long view—evolutionary time—is telescoped into one crucial afternoon. Concomitant with this thematic preoccupation is a practical one: Albee's theatricality requires precision timing, and he can be heard to mutter "*tempi!*" as he watches a production of one of his plays, implying that the scripts are like musical scores. In a published conversation called "Context Is All," Albee suggests this musicality of a play: "You can conduct a play when you're directing it" (*SMM*, 228).

"Calm seas and prosperous voyage"

This line from "Homelife" describes the choice Peter and Ann made of a marriage of safety, a life without storms and without worry—a choice already showing signs of exhaustion before Peter leaves their home to spend his Sunday afternoon, as he always does, reading a book on a bench in Central Park. In Albee's view, it is this very safety that is so dangerous. It is worth noting that his plays have become more and more interested in sexuality as a driving force in human life, as a gauge of vitality. Many of Albee's plays are about heterosexual, long-lasting marriages between sophisticated, middle-aged, well-to-do men and women; despite his own homosexuality, he rarely writes about same-sex relationships. From the start, the plays emphasize the need to acknowledge one's "animal" existence—a belief introduced in the first play, *The Zoo Story*, and evident throughout the rest, in crescendo, until its most literal as well its most metaphoric manifestation in *The Goat*. The underlying urgency of Albee's belief, which fuels all his work, is revealed in a remark made on the radio: "We must stay fully alive knowing full well we are not going to stay alive forever . . . I wish more people would live dangerously" (National Public Radio, September 23, 2004). Living and making art and responding to art are all of a piece for Albee; in his essay "Some Thoughts on Sculpture," he discusses "the illimits of art" and, specifically, a few contemporary sculptors whose work he has acquired for his private collection: "They are all dangerous, in that they do not leave our perceptions unaltered" (*SMM*, 163). One might say the same of Albee's best—and most dangerous—plays.

In his introduction to volume 1 of *The Collected Plays*, Albee writes, "I do not plan out my plays to fit in with either critical bias or commercial safety; nor do I worry that my themes may be difficult or dangerous and my techniques unconventional. I go with what my mind tells me it wants to do, and I take my chances. . . . it gives me freedom for my wisdoms and my follies" (1:8). The dangers of safety are examined in each of Albee's plays, which reveal, in dazzlingly different ways, how crucial it is to live honorably—true to oneself, true to one's art, true to one's ethical and philosophical beliefs. In a television interview with Charlie Rose when *The Goat* was nominated for the Tony Award for Best Play (which it subsequently won), he explained that his theatrical aim is to make "people imagine what they cannot conceive of imagining, to imagine how they would feel if they were in this situation, to learn something about the nature of love, of tolerance, and consciousness." This comment could stand as the headnote to the entire Albee canon.

Peter and Jerry: "Homelife" and The Zoo Story

The Zoo Story, written in 1958, launched Albee's career. And in 2004, nearly half a century later, he would premiere its first act, called "Homelife," adding an umbrella title, *Peter and Jerry*, to the whole work. Albee has indicated that in the future he wants *The Zoo Story* to be performed with this new first act—an immense requirement, considering the frequency with which this classic of the American canon is performed, not to mention the number of anthologies that include *The Zoo Story* as a free-standing play. In this revisiting process, Albee has trimmed the famous script slightly and has updated a few details (i.e., Peter's salary has gone up from eighteen thousand dollars in the original to two hundred thousand dollars, and microwave ovens have been added to the inventory of bourgeois equipment in Peter's apartment).

The Zoo Story opens with Peter, a textbook editor, reading on a bench in Central Park. He is soon joined by Jerry, who tells him bizarre stories about himself, his lewd landlady, and her ferocious dog, whom he tries first to befriend and then to kill. The meeting of the two men will, unlike the meeting of man and dog, have fatal consequences.

The script describes Peter as "a man in his early forties, neither fat nor gaunt, neither handsome nor homely." The description in

"Homelife" calls for a Peter who is "bland; not heavy; pleasant, if uninteresting looking. Tidy; circumspect." It is odd that the descriptions are not identical, since, after all it is the same character and the same day; it is also odd that "circumspect" is not a physical description. But the point is, of course, that Peter is a *type*, not a person: nondescript, tweedy, and timid. This makes it all the more surprising that Albee told the *New York Times*, "I always thought that there was more to the character of Peter. He was seen by many audiences through the eyes of Jerry. I think people will find him now more sympathetic and understandable" (Zinoman, E2). As testimony to Albee's ongoing interest in his first play, he wrote a variation on it called *Another Part of the Zoo* for a private showing at a benefit function in 1981.

In retroactively developing Peter's character, "Homelife" gives us an opening scene in his conventionally tasteful Upper East Side apartment (in the Hartford Stage premiere production this included a blooming orchid plant on a glass-topped coffee table, an oriental carpet, discreet pictures on the walls). When his wife, Ann, walks in, dish towel in hand, saying, "We should talk," he doesn't reply; he doesn't even look up. She exits with dish towel. A few beats later, he suddenly registers what he has heard and says, "What? We should what?"

As anybody who has ever been in a relationship knows—or as anybody who has ever watched an Albee play about marriage recognizes—this is one of those "uh-oh" moments, which is the perfect place to start a play. It is also a funny line, metatheatrically, since Albee's plays are almost all talk, and "We should talk" is an amusingly self-reflexive announcement of the play's beginning.

Much of what transpires in "Homelife" could have been imagined by readers or spectators of *The Zoo Story:* we see the civility, the orderly domesticity, the feminized quality (wife, two daughters, two cats) of Peter's life. What we find out is the question most American plays seek to answer: How did this character get that way? It is all backstory, although the modest triumph of this first-act addition is that "Homelife" transcends the merely expository function.

In the Hartford Stage premiere production, the acts were tied

Peter and Jerry: "Homelife," with Johanna Day and Frank Wood, Hartford Stage, 2004. (Photograph by T. Charles Erickson.)

together in interesting ways: Peter's wife slaps him—to her and his surprise—and in act 2, Jerry slaps him on the same cheek. He sits on the sofa in the apartment exactly where he will sit in act 2 on the park bench, both times absorbed in his book. Ann will do most of the talking in act 1, just as Jerry does most of the talking in act 2. Similar blocking and the pacing is another of the ways a director may stitch the two acts together.

One of the questions always hovering over *The Zoo Story* is why Peter, who is, after all, a New Yorker and therefore presumably used to defending himself against peculiar and talkative strangers, stays and listens to Jerry, and what makes him receptive to this disagreeable man who mocks his lack of sons, his bourgeois lifestyle, and his deficiency of "animal" manhood. "Homelife" answers by showing us why Peter is so vulnerable on this Sunday afternoon. Thus, the new first act shows us not only his bourgeois, materialistic life (which

Peter and Jerry: The Zoo Story, with Frank Wood and Frederick Weller; Hartford Stage, 2004. (Photograph by T. Charles Erickson.)

might make any bookish, liberal New Yorker feel slightly defensive), but, far more important, shows us his wife's sexual frustration. Albee's plays have grown increasingly preoccupied with sexuality, as both crucial to a person's life and an accurate gauge of vitality. Anne reveals her longing for a life more adventurous and passionate than the "calm seas and prosperous voyage" that defines her marriage. The dangers of safety have been a strong, recurrent Albee theme, and we see now why Peter, indicted both by his wife and by himself, psychologically undefended as he leaves his house to go to the park, is susceptible to and gives credence to Jerry's accusations.

Specifically, we learn two important things: first, that Peter is worried about his penis "retreating," and, second, that Peter had an experience when he was in college that altered his sex life permanently. He was pledging a fraternity and at a "sex party" was encouraged to have anal sex with a girl pledging a sorority. His own sexual power and arousal carried him away, and he hurt her badly, creating a bloody scene. Since then he has practiced restraint, the very restraint that has made him a tender but unexciting lover, as he learns (and we learn) from his wife's wistful complaints.

Ann is described as "38 . . . Tall, a bit angular; pleasant-looking, unexceptional." Her bland appearance suggests that Ann and Peter are a well-matched couple. Jerry says that Peter is "a richly comic person," but we feel this is sarcasm or irony; Ann, on the other hand, is genuinely funny:

> ANN. Before I married you my mother said to me, "Why *ever* would you want to marry a man publishes textbooks?"
> PETER. *(Smiles)* She did not.
> ANN. Well, she could have, and maybe she did. "Why *ever* would you want to marry a man publishes textbooks?" "Gee, Ma, *I* don't know—seems like fun."
> PETER. I thought your family liked me.
> ANN. They *do.* "He's a good solid man," Dad said. I've told you this. "None of this . . . fly by night fiction stuff."
> PETER. *(Laughs)* "Fly by night." What does that *mean*? Bats? And how does it relate to fiction?
> ANN. I made it up. He never said it. Look it up. (7)

His literal turn of mind shows in his responses over and over; for example, when Ann pretends to be an obstetrician delivering the son they never had (another phantom Albee baby), saying ,"Well, Sir, that's a fine bouncing baby boy you've got there!" Peter replies, "I've never understood 'bouncing'. They don't . . . bounce it, do they? To see if . . ." (32).

During their conversation about Ann's insomnia, we register her dismay when she discovers he has always known about her sleep-lessness but has never worried about her state of mind or inquired as to why she gets out of bed. Her taunting but specifically "not accusatory" suggestions—that she could go out into the street and scream, or strip and lie down and "spread [her] legs to the night" are met with a deprecatory smile and a "No; you wouldn't." His error comes from his complacent explanation as to why he has never fol-lowed her in her predawn wanderings: "Enough to know it doesn't matter, that there's nothing wrong." But of course there is something wrong.

After a bizarre conversation about her breasts and his circumcision, she remarks, "It's not your subject."

PETER. What?
ANN. Sex stuff.
PETER. No; I guess not.
ANN. *(An assessment, but not unkind)* Mr. Circumspection. (28)

This last wry appraisal picks up the word "circumspect" from Albee's original description of Peter in *The Zoo Story*.

When they return to the opening gambit—Ann's feeling they "should talk," Peter assumes she had nothing "important," or "threatening" or "terrible" in mind. Ann says, "And we don't *have* that, *do* we?" Peter replies with a sigh, "No. But—as you say—we're probably going to, one day." This is clearly the moment that foreshadows *The Zoo Story*, in which the "threatening" and the "terrible" do indeed occur. And rather too explicitly, she will later say, "But where's the . . . the rage, the . . . animal? [. . .] Why don't we behave like that . . . like beasts?! [. . .] we're too . . . civilized?" (48). And after she hears his story of the fraternity party, the easy cause-and-effect of his sexual restraint, she tells him, "That must be what I wanted—a little . . . disorder around here, a little . . . chaos" (57).

Exit Peter to read in Central Park. Enter Jerry and chaos when, after intermission, *The Zoo Story* begins.

The Zoo Story

As a way of explaining his circuitous route to Central Park, Jerry tells Peter, "Sometimes a person has to go a very long distance out of his way to come back a short distance correctly" (1:21). This cryptic line seems a perfect explanation for the odd fact that *The Zoo Story* premiered in Berlin in 1959.

In *The Zoo Story*, Jerry starts a conversation with Peter that becomes more and more intense and unnerving as he describes his repulsive landlady, her belligerent dog (which he tries first to befriend and then to murder), and the other marginalized denizens of the zoolike tenement he lives in as a "permanent transient," a phrase more descriptive of an existential condition than an address. The zoo is the play's central symbol, the place where wild creatures are confined, where bars separate the animals from each other and from the people watching, "But, if it's a zoo, that's the way it is" (1:34). By extension, the thin walls of the tenement building function in much the same way, and the invisible bars that separate people from people extend the metaphor to the world as we live in it, the cages we all inhabit, whether the bars are socioeconomic or political, emotional or psychological. Consider, too, the self-reflexive notion that theater itself is zoolike: audiences are separated from the actors on stage, and we watch the creatures who perform for our entertainment, passively observing the lives they enact, often with a sense of superiority and the security of distance.

It is curious to note that the same image of the zoo occurs in Arthur Miller's *All My Sons*, written a dozen years earlier; near the end of that play, Chris, desperately arguing with his fiancée about his father's immoral decision to ship damaged goods during the war, a decision that saved his business and killed many young pilots, tells her of his horror at what postwar society has become: "This is the land of the great big dogs, you don't love a man here, you eat him! That's the principle; the only one we live by—it just happened to kill a few people this time, that's all. The world's that way, how can I take it out on him? What sense does that make? This is a zoo, a zoo!" (66). Miller's morality is more stridently expressed than Albee's, but the same protest informs both plays, expressed in the same zoo image: the collapse of a vital American community under the weight of materialism, the betrayal of the social contract, and the consequent damage to the human spirit.

The fundamental characteristic of bourgeois society is ownership, and Jerry's challenge of Peter's claim to the bench is the catalystic event. Jerry finally shoves Peter off the bench, challenging him to fight for it, tossing him a knife. When Peter, stunned and terrified, holds the knife out to ward Jerry off, Jerry impales himself on it and Peter runs away saying, "Oh my God."

The great question of the play remains: what happens when Peter goes home? Of course, if Albee had written a sequel instead of a prequel, our interpretive pleasures would be ruined. It is the very multivalence of the play's meaning, the suggestive provocations of the script, that keep this play freshly shocking. Audience members may still walk out in self-protective disgust or confusion.

Following are some interpretations of *The Zoo Story* a reader or theatergoer might entertain:

If we read the play as a sociopolitical critique, it is an indictment of corrupt American society where materialism instead of humanism has become the prevailing value, preferring the acquisition of stuff to expressions of love. The bench thus becomes emblematic of territory, as well as property, which, if read sociologically, suggests the "have-nots" violently displacing the "haves." Peter discovers through Jerry's guidance that bourgeois civilization is the zoo we all live in, some cages being better furnished than others; Peter discovers his own animal nature—violent and shocking—the very animal nature "Homelife" shows us he has been repressing all these years. The threatened failure of the American Dream and the consequent lethal definition of success in capitalist terms is a familiar theme in twentieth-century American drama, obvious from a consideration of the classics: *Long Day's Journey Into Night, Death of a Salesman, A Raisin in the Sun, Cat on a Hot Tin Roof, Fences,* and *True West.* Since Peter is the play's neutral Everyman, he is the character the middle-class audience is most likely to identify with (in *The Zoo Story,* moreso than in "Homelife"—and this may be a problem in the addition of a first act, where we tend to identify and sympathize with Ann); it is thus our values that are assaulted by Jerry, and *The Zoo Story* becomes a cautionary tale.

If we read the play as a Christian allegory, Jerry is a Jesus figure (this can be emphasized by the director or the actor's choosing a crucified posture in death on the bench) who dies to "save" Peter. Thus Peter's exit line, "OH MY GOD!" heard offstage as a "pitiful howl" becomes resonant with meaning. This is intensified by Jerry's final line, delivered, the stage directions tell us, with "scornful mimicry and supplication" as he ends the play with "Oh . . . my . . . God." The biblical implications here are immense. After Jerry impales himself, Peter whispers, "Oh my God, oh my God, oh my God" and Jerry, in his death throes, says, "I came unto you," adding, in reversal of expectation, "and you have comforted me. Dear Peter." Peter's name now seems more significant.

If we read the play as an existential allegory, Jerry gives life meaning by choosing death, and, consequentially forces choice and thereby meaning in Peter's life; the loss of the bench suggests that Peter has been forcibly wrenched out of his comfortable, insulated life to become *engagé.*

If we read the play's conclusion as pessimistic, we discover that *The Zoo Story* demonstrates that meaningful contact between people is impossible, and that Jerry's longing is hopeless as well as preposterous. The only outcome is the "assisted suicide," and thus the entire play is a setup: Jerry was looking for someone to help him prove the impossibility of communicating with another person and the further impossibility of living a fulfilling life. This interpretation is also a way of making sense of his isolated existence, despite being surrounded by people.

If we read the play's conclusion as optimistic, we discover that Peter has been freed from his civilized shell, and recovered his animal identity, relinquishing the "vegetable" life that had imprisoned him in safety. Thus, communication between people *is* possible, and Peter is initiated into true manhood. The male competition that informs so many American plays has been oddly transformed here from the faux violence of the locker room (what Sam Shepard in *True West* calls "snappin' towels at each other's privates") to the real violence here of the knifing. This leads to the odd and dismaying speculation that, if this theory is followed to its logical conclusion, the play demonstrates that standing up for his manhood means that homicide is preferable to passivity, echoing Jerry's provocation: "You fight for your self-respect; you fight for that goddamned bench. [. . .] fight for your manhood, you pathetic little vegetable" (1:38). Thus Jerry's aggression might make him the most recognizably American of the two.

If we read the play as a homosexual allegory, it redefines the meeting between the two men. Frequently, readers assume that Jerry is homosexual and that this is a Central Park pickup gone very wrong. If one entertains this idea, it suggests that Peter's unresolved homosexual inclination is what enables the play—that is why he stays and listens to Jerry. This would explain why he is, sexually, an unenthusiastic husband, and why Jerry is so repulsed by his landlady's lewd interest. The bizarre tickling scene contributes to this interpretation.

Tickling is the perfect emblem for the interaction between the two men, whether we see it as a surrogate for homosexual interaction or as an emblem of social interaction, since despite the laughter it causes, tickling is an assertion of power; only the tickler is enjoying, however perversely, the situation, while the person being tickled generally feels desperate and powerless and foolish. During the tickling scene, Peter loses his grip and, "beside himself" with his "own mad whimsy," babbles "the parakeets will be getting dinner ready soon. . . . And the cats are setting the table," all the tokens of his feminized, heterosexual life. The point of it all is, "I had my own zoo there for a moment" (1:33). If Peter's stabbing of Jerry is viewed as a homosexual act of penetration, Peter has discovered the truth of his animal nature.

Finally (and of course this is only final as the last item in this brief list), if we read the play as a psychological allegory, it is possible to view it as a monodrama: Jerry and Peter are two sides of the same person, and the internal conflict has been made theatrically manifest. If we follow this notion to its conclusion, it suggests that Peter kills his wild, nonconformist side (the rebel-without-a-cause lurking under the three-piece suit), this, too, is a grim conclusion: the triumph of the bourgeoisie. On the other hand, it more could be more positively said that Peter, in standing up for himself (literally as well as figuratively), finds his identity and resolves his inner division. If Jerry is that part of Peter which embodies the self-accusation that he is a vegetable, echoing Ann's accusation that Peter is too civilized, will he then return home to give Ann what she craves? Or has he stifled/ murdered that suspicion about himself, to return home to become the fully docile husband, unconflicted and unhappy? In either case, the play, with the addition of its first act, becomes another marriage play, as so many of Albee's plays are.

The Death of Bessie Smith

Although this short play is rarely revived, it is worth discussing (and reviving, for that matter) for several reasons: first, although it is unlike Albee's other work in that it has an overt sociopolitical agenda (Brechtian by his own assessment), that very agenda sheds light on the less overt sociopolitical concerns that run through his other work. In this eight-scene one-act, the plot focuses neither on Bessie Smith nor her death in a car crash, but on the southern, racist world in which she dies, denied help from an all-white hospital, as the legend goes. The counterpoint between the world of the hospital and the brief glimpses of Bessie and Jack as they approach that world, indicates that Albee's interest is on the corrosive effects of racism rather than on the famous singer's death, despite the play's title.

The Death of Bessie Smith is different from Albee's other work stylistically as well, in that it depends heavily on lighting for meaning and effect—and lighting designers rarely get much to do in an Albee play since his theatrical arena is, typically, verbal rather than visual. As is frequently the case in Albee's plays, none of the characters in *The Death of Bessie Smith* is particularly admirable or even likable; the vision that informs this work is deeply pessimistic about the human capacity for decency and sympathy, but, significantly, Albee makes us feel sympathy for his imperfect people.

To begin at the end: the play's final image speaks its meaning. Stage directions tell us, "The room fades into silhouette again. . . . The great sunset blazes; music up." Recall Peter Brook's remarkable dictum in *The Empty Space:*

> I know of one acid test in the theatre. . . . When a performance is over, what remains? Fun can be forgotten, but powerful emotion also disappears and good arguments lose their thread. When emotion and argument are harnessed to a wish from the audience to see more clearly into itself—then something in the mind burns. The event scorches on to the memory an outline, a taste, a trace, a smell, a picture. It is the play's central image that remains, its silhouette, and if the elements are rightly blended this silhouette will be its meaning, this shape will be the essence of what it has to say. (136)

The truth of *The Death of Bessie Smith* lies in that silhouette—a significantly black-and-white image; these characters—the white nurse frozen in shock at having been slapped, the black orderly, his "back to the wall"—both silhouetted against the blazing sunset: both races are caught, and the symbolic sunset ends this day and this era, as well as Bessie Smith's life, as well as the play. The Intern, supposedly the idealist of the play, has been exposed as a covert materialist: he longs for the mayor's fancy Cord automobile. His girlfriend of convenience, the Nurse, replies with contempt, "Cord automobiles and . . . and sunsets . . . those are . . . fine preoccupations. Is that what you think about? Huh? Driving a fine car into a fine sunset?" (1:66), an image that suggests both escape and demise. It is worth remembering at this point that the Nurse's impassioned speech of disgust in scene 8 ends with "I am tired of my skin" (1:74), suggesting that not only is she tired of her self and her existence, but, implicitly, that she is tired of the sociopolitical burden of being white. That these characters are all trapped in and by their skin is crucial to the play's thematic indictment of racism. The Intern's mocking speech to the nurse who has mocked his appreciation of the sunset is significant: "The west is burning . . ." The image suggests conflagration rather than natural beauty, a preamble to George's prophecy-of-doom speech, reading from Spengler's *Decline of the West* in *Who's Afraid of Virginia*

Woolf? The Intern's comment, "It's a truly beautiful sight," is both radical and wry if we think of the sun setting on this nasty and cruel world driven by racism.

Scene 3 ends with Jack's urging an offstage Bessie to get out of bed so they can get on the road; it is important to note that Bessie Smith never appears in the play—the play is not really about the singer but about the contextual society. Jack reassures her that although they need to keep the appointment with "that bastard" (presumably John Hammond) for Bessie to make a comeback, she need not feel trapped: "I told him you was free as a bird, honey. Free as a goddamn bird" (1:53). The irony of this image is obvious: no black woman, not even the Empress of the Blues, was "free as a bird" in the Deep South in 1937. His monologue ends with the hopeful, "We're goin' north again!" as "the lights fade on this scene" and "the sunset is predominant" (1:54). The scene continues briefly with no one onstage; Jack's voice is heard ("O.K.; here we go; we're on our way") as the sound of a car fades away and "the sunset dims again." The visuals tell us about the inevitability of the action that will follow, even if the audience or reader does not know the Bessie Smith legend.

The play begins with an evocation—conscious or not—of Tennessee Williams; Jack meets old friend Bernie in a bar and is eager to brag about his connection with Bessie Smith. His coy answer to Bernie's "What you *doin'* here?" is, "Oh, travelin'; travelin'." This echoes Blanche's famous line near the beginning of *A Streetcar Named Desire:* "Traveling wears me out." Williams's play, written thirteen years earlier, is echoed again when the Nurse and the Intern are quarrelling in scene 6 and he says, "Your family is a famous *name,* but those thousand acres are *gone,* and the pillars of your house are blistered and flaking" (1:68). Both plays, to some extent, address the transition between the Old South and the New South, the postwar world where plantations and antebellum balls were quaint relics of a life no longer livable. This is the only play of Albee's set in the South, and it is likely that the young playwright, living in New York, might have acquired his southern geography and his characters' rhythms of speech from his already-famous and deeply southern predecessor.

But despite their southernness, these characters sound like Albee characters, and reading *The Death of Bessie Smith* with his later, greater plays in mind, the similarities are unmistakable. The black Orderly is Albee's word man—there are always characters in his plays who are highly attuned to language—although the Orderly's speech is often stilted with a formality that curries favor in all the wrong ways. When the Nurse seems to mock the hospital's even-handed treatment of the mayor with hemorrhoids and a man dying of a stab wound, the Orderly chuckles, "I like your contempt." And although contempt was exactly what the Nurse was expressing, she becomes incensed with the Orderly for attempting to share it, and he reasonably replies, "Why, it's a matter of proportion. Surely you don't *condone* the fact that the mayor and his piles and that *poor* man lying up there . . . ?" Her tongue-lashing begins: "*Condone!* Will you listen to that: condone: My! Aren't you the educated one. What . . . what does that word mean, boy? That word condone? Hunh? You do talk some, don't you?" (1:55). Albee's emphasizing of the word "condone" carries much of the meaning of the play and explains exactly why the Orderly's ambition and education, considered inap-propriate in this racist environment, are mingled with his self-pro-tective obsequiousness. When the Nurse asks, "Whatever do you expect?" he replies, "What's been promised. . . . Nothing more. Just that. [. . .] there are some people who believe in more than promises; there are some people who believe in action" (1:56). This foreshad-ows the Nurse's response when Jack bursts into the emergency room and is told to wait, just as he was told to "wait" and "cool his heels" at the first hospital. Wait, Albee seems to be saying, is what the white world had been telling the black world in the United States to do, keeping in mind that the play takes place in a pre–Civil Rights Act Mississippi.

But there is no triumphant agenda here, since Albee proceeds to compromise each of the his characters so that no one carries the weight of the playwright's social outrage. The Orderly, who "tries to please everybody," has "Uncle Tom'd" himself out of both worlds, so that he is "now an inhabitant of no-man's land, on the one side shunned and disowned by your brethren, and on the other an object of contempt and derision to your betters" (1:59). The Intern is more concerned with the Spanish Civil War than with local suffering caused by local oppression, although it is probably to his credit that unlike the Nurse's attitude toward the mayor, Bessie Smith is not a celebrity to him, but merely "this woman." The Father is a blowhard racist, and his daughter, the Nurse, is so conflicted socially, sexually, and politically that all she wants is escape—something no Albee character achieves. The rhythms and language of the Nurse's speech anticipate Martha's; when she threatens the Intern with, "You have done it, boy [. . .] I am going to get you. . . . I am going to fix you . . . I am going to see to it that you are *through* here [. . .] You have over-stepped yourself . . . and you are going to wish you hadn't. I'll get my father" (1:68–69), she sounds much like Martha threatening George, two infuriated women, each with a powerful father. A bit later she sounds like Martha talking to Nick: "Yeah . . . I think I'd like that . . . keep both of you jumping. I *would* like coffee, and I *would* like you to get it for me. So why don't you just trot right across the hall and get me some?" (1:71).

The Nurse's despair and disgust are metaphysical rather than political, which is what keeps Albee closer to Beckett than to Miller, whose plays deeply believe in the possibility of social remediation. When she shouts at the Orderly, she shouts out Albee's vision:

> I am sick of it! I am *sick.* I am sick of everything in this hot, stupid, fly-ridden *world.* I am sick of the disparity between things as they are, and as they should be! [. . .] I am sick of going to bed and I am sick of waking up . . . I am tired . . . I am tired of the truth . . . and I am tired of lying about the truth . . . I am tired of my skin . . . I WANT OUT! (1:74)

Nobody in an Albee play every gets "out"; there is no escape from self.

Albee's inspiration for the writing of the play came from a record album cover:

> I had loved gospel music and early jazz for a long time. I used to hear those Gospel shows Off-Broadway and Off-Off-Broadway in the

fifties. . . . I'd also been listening to Bessie Smith's records. An LP had come out and I happened to read on the album cover the story of how she died, the automobile accident outside of Memphis, her arm outside the window of the car, her arm almost cut off, how she was taken to a white hospital and was refused admission and died on the way to a second hospital. That generated the play. How long after I became aware of that information did I write it? It can't have been very long. I made the necessary additional step, the gift of the dead Bessie Smith to the second hospital. That was totally my invention. But those facts prompted the play. (*ASJ,* 99)

But these are not the "facts" about her death, as subsequent discoveries and confessions have revealed, and it is surprising that, apparently, neither Albee nor Gussow, his biographer, bothered to pursue the facts beyond the album cover in all the decades between the writing of the play and the writing of the biography. In his astute commentary on this play, C. W. E. Bigsby writes, "Over and above the level of social protest this is a play about individuals trapped in their own myths" (260), and that trap is larger than he knew, since Bigsby, too, accepts the myth of Bessie Smith's death without question, as though playwrights were reliable sources of historical information (cf. Shakespeare's "history" plays!).

A more reliable account is available in Chris Albertson's biography *Bessie,* written in 1972 while some of the significant sources of information were still alive (she died in 1937), and substantiated by many other versions of the story. Albertson describes the origins of the legend of her death: In an article published in *downbeat* magazine, John Hammond, the record company executive who was her producer, said that Smith had been denied treatment in a whites-only Mississippi hospital because she was black (Hammond was expecting to make a handsome profit on her records when he reissued them). This was the story that Albee read on the album cover. Hammond later withdrew his story, admitting that it was based on rumor.

The drama over these allegations continued when in an online essay Gail Jarvis denounced Albee's play and its premise. Jarvis pointed out that no white ambulance driver at that time in that place would have taken a black woman to a white hospital. The claim that

Smith had died while the ambulance was "racing across the State of Mississipi desperately trying to find a black hospital" makes no sense since Clarksdale's black hospital was less than a mile away from the white hospital. In a newspaper account from 1938, the ambulance driver said he took Smith to the black hospital and that she was dead on arrival (Albertson, 222–25). Jarvis insists that Albee fanned the flames of scapegoating white Southerners in the climate of the times: in 1954 the Supreme Court outlawed school segregation; in 1957 troops were sent to Little Rock, and John F. Kennedy made campaign headlines when he telephoned Martin Luther King in jail.

Other elements of the play are also at odd with the facts: for example, the man who was driving the car that crashed and who appears in the hospital and thus onstage is named Jack. Bessie Smith's husband was named Jack Gee, but she had been estranged from him for seven years. Jack Gee left their adopted son, Jack Gee, Jr., behind in New York instead of taking him to Bessie's funeral in Philadelphia, claiming there was no room in the car. The man she was traveling with was Richard Morgan.

Pinkas Braun, a Swiss actor who read Albee's script with some thought of producing it for German television, extends Jarvis's dispute over the facts to include the play's larger purposes. Braun wrote to Albee explaining his view of its glaring flaw:

> It makes it so easy for everybody in the audience to say, "These awful people. How could they ever allow themselves to let such a terrible thing happen? If Bessie would have come to us, we would have saved her; she might still be living." And this cannot be what you wanted. In my opinion you wanted to brand the phantom prejudice which haunts our society and with which almost everybody is at least a little bit "sicklied o'er." . . . You should not take for granted that people know her and know her destiny. You should try to make the audience understand the tragic measures of this human failure. (*ASJ*, 133)

Albee wrote back, acknowledging the validity of Braun's criticism and vowing to work on the play until "I have done what I wanted to do," extending it beyond "sociological values." The revised version, which added the first two scenes, was then sent to Albee's friend the composer Ned Rorem (to whom the play is dedicated), who responded, "As a play now it dazzles with terror" (*ASJ*, 134). The "terror" of the "human failure" is what the play achieves, facts notwithstanding.

It is surprising that Albee does not specify what music is to be played, although his stage directions require it. If the director attempts a realistic production, which will probably wrench the play out of shape, he may choose music that suits the time and taste of the characters. If the play is to be a lament, as well as a protest, recordings of Bessie Smith are appropriate. Of all the blues songs Bessie Smith wrote and sang, "Long Old Road" seems to provide perfect underscoring for this play:

> It's a long old road, but I'm gonna find the end
> It's a long old road, but I'm gonna find the end
> And when I get there I'm gonna shake hands with a friend
>
> On the side of the road I sat underneath a tree
> On the side of the road I sat underneath a tree
> Nobody knows the thought that came over me.
>
> Weepin' and cryin', tears fallin' on the ground
> Weepin' and cryin', tears fallin' on the ground
> When I got to the end I was so worried down
>
> Picked up my bag, baby, and I tried again
> Picked up my bag, baby, and I tried again
> I got to make it, I've got to find the end
>
> You can't trust nobody, you might as well be alone
> You can't trust nobody, you might as well be alone
> Found my long lost friend and I might as well stayed at home.
>
> (Davis, 308)

The Sandbox

This very short—its playing time is fourteen minutes—and very early play is, in several ways, typical of Albee's work. It might be called Albee's first family drama. Following as it does both *The Zoo Story* and *The Death of Bessie Smith*, *The Sandbox* continues Albee's critique of American society, indicting bourgeois values and the cruelties licensed by privilege. Further, *The Sandbox* continues Albee's inclination to leave his characters unnamed, making them embodiments of their life roles rather than particularized individuals.

The Sandbox (1960) metamorphosed a year later into *The American Dream*, where Mommy, Daddy, Grandma, and the Young Man meet again as the tiny *Sandbox* grew into a one-act. In his 1960 preface to the Signet edition, Albee explains the chronology of composition: the start of his writing of *The American Dream* preceded *The Sandbox*, which he wrote "to satisfy a commission from the Festival of Two Worlds" in Spoleto, Italy; "I extracted several of the characters from *The American Dream* and placed them in a situation different than, but related to, their predicament in the longer play. They seem happy out of doors, in *The Sandbox,* and I hope they will not be distressed back in a stuffy apartment, in *The American Dream.*"

Mommy and Daddy are designed to be contemptible: Albee warns us in the play's prefatory note that their names are "of empty affection and point up the pre-senility and vacuity of their characters." Mommy is devoid of sympathy for her mother and respect for her husband; she wields her power ruthlessly and unthinkingly, although she is hypocritically gracious and slightly flirtatious with nonfamily characters. Daddy, "a small man; gray, thin," is ineffectual and "whining." Emblematically, they represent the new couple: domineering woman and passive, emasculated man—a theme that recurs with subtle complexity in *Who's Afraid of Virginia Woolf?* Of all the characters, only Grandma, "a tiny, wizened woman with bright eyes," is sympathetic and interesting. As a personality, her appeal springs from her feistiness and sarcasm; Mommy and Daddy hear only her senile cries of "Ahhhhhh!" and "Graaaa!" while she bangs her toy shovel, but we have access to the person still alive and well inside, the woman who speaks directly to the audience.

This device—one of the play's many violations of the theatrical conventions of fourth-wall realism—functions in several ways: first, it creates sympathy for the character who has been brought to the beach to die, unceremoniously dumped into a sandbox, which is, of course, a redundancy on a beach, but this is just one of the play's many absurdities. The title of the play calls attention to the sociological satire created by this image. Part of Albee's outrage is Grandma's infantilization by her daughter, and by extension, the treatment of old people in American society. Grandma tells us that they moved her into their house, "fixed a nice place for me under the stove . . . gave me an army blanket . . . and my own dish . . . my very own dish!" (1:91). She has been treated like a dog and now is treated like a child, while we, the readers or audience, know that the interior Grandma is alert and sarcastic and amusing. She charms us, so we identify entirely with the victim and not the victimizers. A realistic play about this situation (so prevalent today as people live longer and exceed their capacity to live independently) might evenhandedly reveal the distress on both sides, both parent and child. But Albee is interested in indictment, not in fairness. Perhaps the beach represents an old-age home and the sandbox represents a coffin or a grave—in which Grandma is supposed to help bury herself.

The American family drama is also the American social drama:

just as Grandma's rural past has given her stamina and a sense of humor—both distinctly lacking in the next generation—so rural America's vitality has been overtaken by suburban materialism ("money, money, money"). Lovelessness and selfishness are the dominant characteristics in this smug American way of life, especially the privileging of youth over age, and thus the devaluation of experiential wisdom. Written in the late 1950s, *The Sandbox* is very much a product of Albee's disgust with the self-satisfied prosperous culture of that era. The play has obvious autobiographical roots; its dedication reads, "In memory of my grandmother (1876–1959)." Grandma is named from a grandchild's (i.e., Albee's) perspective; for Mommy and Daddy she would be "Mother," and they seem to have no children to call Grandma "Grandma."

It is worth noting the similarity between Mommy, who, the list of players tells us, is "Fifty-five. A well-dressed, imposing woman," not unlike B of *Three Tall Women*, although far less likable. In that later play, B is fifty-two, the middle-aged version of A, Albee's mother, who when young is called C. Since *The Sandbox* is Albee writing as a much younger man, he was obviously more resentful of her than he would be several decades later, when he wrote *Three Tall Women*. Even more intriguing is that each play also has a character called "the Young Man"; in *Three Tall Women*, he is A's son, which is to say, the playwright's surrogate, making *The Sandbox*'s Young Man all the more shocking in retrospect since he is not only a twenty-five-year-old hunk in a bathing suit, but is also the Angel of Death. He is not silent, as is his counterpart in *Three Tall Women*, but he is fatuous and vacant, a Hollywood actor who is purely a product of a movie studio. When Grandma asks him his name, he replies, "I don't know [. . .] I mean . . . I mean, they haven't given me one yet . . . the studio" (1:91).

As the social mirrors the personal, the theatrical mirrors the societal, just as they always have in drama, although *The Sandbox* is anything but a conventional play. As I have mentioned elsewhere in this volume, late Albee resembles late Beckett (see my comparison between *Three Tall Women* and *Rockaby*), just as early Albee resembles early Beckett—although the similarities are not always obvious.

Waiting for Godot's influence on twentieth-century drama cannot be overstated: for the style and the structure of their major works, playwrights as disparate as Tom Stoppard, Harold Pinter, Athol Fugard, and Suzan-Lori Parks are in Beckett's debt. *The Sandbox* may be the first of Albee's plays to show that effect (although a shaky case can be made for *The Zoo Story*). *The Sandbox* is the first of Albee's plays to employ the techniques of the theater of the absurd, insisting as it does on the concrete stage image rather than realistic illusion and the devices of explanation and what Beckett called "explicitation." A crucial similarity to *Godot* is Albee's metaphysical interest in the manipulation of time, as time passes both quickly (especially in a play lasting less than a quarter of an hour) and slowly as Mommy and Daddy sit on the beach, having deposited Grandma into her sandbox. The following passage is vividly Beckettian:

> DADDY. *(Pause)* What do we do now?
> MOMMY. *(As if remembering)* We . . . wait. We . . . sit here . . . and we wait . . . that's what we do.
> DADDY. *(After a pause)* Shall we talk to each other?
> MOMMY: *(With that little laugh; picking something off her dress)* Well, *you* can talk, if you want to . . . if you can think of anything to say . . . if you can think of anything *new*.
> DADDY. *(Thinks)* No . . . I suppose not.
> MOMMY. *(With a triumphant laugh)* Of course not! (1:89)

This is distilled *Godot*, echoing—almost word for word—many of the exchanges between Vladimir and Estragon as they wait for Godot to come. Mommy's challenge to Daddy, to say something "new," is more than just matrimonial boredom and contempt; the impossibility of saying anything new is, as Beckett demonstrated, the human condition, which he demonstrated by saying, theatrically, something very new.

A bit further along in *The Sandbox*, there is a brief exchange about waiting. Mommy and Daddy have waited, presumably, through the long day (lights go from "brightest day" to "deepest night," according to Albee's scene directions, although this happens in just a few moments of stage time:

DADDY. *(Stirring)* It's nighttime.
MOMMY. Shhh. Be still . . . wait.
DADDY. *(Whining)* It's so hot.
MOMMY. Shhhhhh. Be still . . . wait. (1:91)

This last line will be repeated several times by the Young Man talk-ing to Grandma as she dies, implying the inevitability of mortality. It would also seem to imply Albee's interpretation of *Waiting for Godot:* the Godot whom Didi and Gogo are waiting for is death—one of the many ways of reading that noncharacter who creates a non-event by not arriving but who always promises to arrive tomorrow. If human life can be defined as a long wait for the end, *The Sandbox* takes up this theme as the Young Man tells Grandma, "Shhhh . . . be very still." And then he explains, "I am the Angel of Death. I am . . . uh . . . I am come for you." He delivers the line "like a real amateur," according to Albee's stage directions (1:94), suggesting that even this momentous event is fake, and not even a good fake; the Young Man is only good looking, having no talent and no substance. This Angel of Death is merely a faux Godot, but, just as we are about to find the scene funny, real death overtakes Grandma, and the script turns on a dime. Grandma mocks Mommy and Daddy's fatuous and self-con-gratulatory "It pays to do things well" (1:93), and then when she bravely tries to sit up, she finds she cannot move; suddenly the play is deeply moving.

The "reality" of her death is, of course, heightened by the fact that the actor playing Grandma is acting; consider in comparison Tom Stoppard's scene in *Rosencrantz & Guildenstern are Dead* (another Son-of-Sam play in *Godot*'s debt) when the company of players, on their way to Elsinore, demonstrate various stage deaths. Guildenstern argues that "you scream and choke and sink to your knees but it doesn't bring death home to anyone—it doesn't catch them unawares and start the whisper in their skulls that says—'One day you are going to die.'" The Player replies, "On the contrary, it's the only kind they do believe. . . . Audiences know what to expect, and that is all they are prepared to believe in." Like any actor in a self-reflexive play, Grandma has to give the audience that double consciousness, both that "whisper" and the artistic awareness of the acting. Albee's stage directions resonate when Mommy and Daddy, rejoicing that their "long night is over," go to look at Grandma, who "plays dead"—and Albee follows that stage direction with a gleeful exclamation point (1:93).

The Sandbox, like *Waiting for Godot* and *Rosencrantz & Guildenstern are Dead*, is filled with playful reminders to the audience that this is a play: lighting cues ("Don't put the lights up yet . . . I'm not ready; I'm not quite ready"), sound cues ("It was an off-stage rumble, and you know what *that* means"), dialogue cues ("Uh . . . ma'am; I . . . I have a line here") and critical comments ("You did that very well, dear"). The music is more complicated; the characters list includes a Musician, and although Albee specifies "No particular age, but young would be nice," he does not specify the instrument, as long as it can be played from a chair with a music stand. The musical accompaniment suggests Mommy's funeral arrangements and simultaneously provides the underscoring of the play. Even though Mommy dismisses the Musician—Grandma is dead, and they exit—he remains onstage until the end, and "continues to play as the curtain slowly comes down."

Finally, the fact that the Angel of Death is merely a Hollywood actor—and not a good one at that—suggests that the self-reflexive theatricality in *The Sandbox* is a comment on the movies that will—maybe—be the Angel of Death to the theater. But like Grandma, the fabulous invalid is not dead yet.

The American Dream

Albee was working on *The American Dream* when he was commissioned to write a short piece for the Festival of Two Worlds in Spoleto, Italy; he used some of the same characters from *American Dream* for the play for Spoleto, which became the *The Sandbox,* and then returned to his one-act. The plot, if so absurdist a play can be said to have one, concerns Mommy and Daddy, who have called Mrs. Barker to their apartment which they share with a still feisty and still abused Grandma and her blind Pekinese. They summon her to express dissatisfaction with their "bumble of joy," adopted, "bought," twenty years earlier. Mommy and Daddy's fatuousness is compounded by their cruelty; the cataloguing of the boy's dismemberment, from eye-gouging to castration, caused Whitney Balliett, reviewing for *The New Yorker*, to write that the play "reach[es] directly back to the butchery and perversion of the Greek theatre" (February 4, 1961: 62, 64), an interesting comment, especially in light of Albee's *The Goat*, another play redolent of ancient Greek "butchery and perversion," and written nearly half a century later.

The autobiographical subtext of the play is, fairly obviously, the revenge of the playwright on his adoptive parents. In addition to Albee's loathing and contempt for Mommy and Daddy is his sympathy for Grandma. The character is "a cameo tribute" to Albee's own maternal grandmother who lived with Albee's parents and kept Pekinese dogs; she not live to see a play of her grandson's performed. In the play, Grandma fears "the van man," and lives under the threat of expulsion from the family home; she packs up her memories in beautifully wrapped boxes in anticipation of being carted away. This placing of horror within a seemingly blithe comic context is signature Albee.

When the Young Man arrives at Mommy and Daddy's home looking for work, Grandma assumes he is "the van man," but it turns out he is the identical twin of an adopted son murdered by Mommy and Daddy. The Young Man had suffered his twin's agonies vicariously, and he and the old woman form an alliance; Albee felt that he and his grandmother were "two ends against the middle" (*ASJ*, 33). It is curious to note that Harold Pinter's famous play *The Birthday Party* (1957, first performed 1958) has a character called Meg, an older woman who runs the seaside boardinghouse in which the action takes place; she is also deeply attached to a young man who plays surrogate son, and Meg's abiding fear is that the "van" will come and she will be taken away.

The result of the Young Man's having sympathetically experienced his brother's mutilation is that he feels "loss," a watchword in Albee's drama, first introduced in *The Zoo Story* when Jerry learns the great lesson of maturity: "what is gained is loss." The Young Man—as beautiful and vacant as his namesake is in *The Sandbox*—has discovered that his heart,

> became numb [. . .] and from that time I have been unable to love. [. . .] there are more losses, but it all comes down to this; I no longer have the capacity to feel anything. [. . .] I let people love me. . . . I accept the syntax around me, for, while I know I cannot relate . . . I know I must be related *to*. I let people love me . . . I let people touch me . . . I let them draw pleasure from my groin . . . from my presence . . . from the fact of me . . . but, that is all it comes to. (1:138–39)

As Grandma says, commenting on his beauty, "You're the American Dream, that's what you are," and shortly after he replies, "I'll do almost anything for money." Thus Albee's indictment—social, cultural, familial—is complete.

In his essay on Eugene Ionesco Albee acknowledges his debt:

> As Pinter's debt to Beckett can be found in much of his work, my own stylistic sources for *The American Dream* and *The Sandbox* are clearly to be found in Ionesco. (Indeed, the first several pages of *The American Dream* were so obviously an intended homage to the Romanian-French master that I was startled when some critics insisted it was an imitation—an Ionesco-like situation?) (*SMM*, 145)

Martin Esslin calls *The American Dream* the "promising and brilliant first example of an American contribution to the Theatre of the Absurd" in his landmark work of that title (313), noting the resemblance to Ionesco's absurdist plays in "its masterly use of clichés," clichés "as characteristically American as Ionesco's are French." The fundamental premises of the theater of the absurd, as set forth by Esslin, who coined the label, go far toward elucidating *The American Dream*. In brief, they include "the sense that the certitudes and unshakable basic assumptions of former ages have been swept away, that they have been tested and found wanting, that they have been discredited as cheap and somewhat childish illusions." Such plays "express . . . the senselessness of the human condition and the inadequacy of the rational approach by the open abandonment of rational devices and discursive thought." "The Theatre of the Absurd has renounced arguing *about* the absurdity of the human condition; it merely *presents* it in being—that is in terms of concrete stage images" (23–25).

The certitude that is here "discredited as [a] cheap and somewhat childish illusion" is the American Dream itself. The first instance of the phrase (thanks due here to Professor Susan Harris Smith) occurs in James Truslow Adams's *The Epic of America* (1931), wherein he defines that "dream of a land in which life should be better and richer and fuller for every man, with opportunity for each according to his ability or his achievement. . . .The American dream that lured tens of millions of all nations to our shores . . . has not been a dream of merely material plenty. . . . It has been a dream of being able to grow to fullest development as man and woman . . . unhampered by the barriers which had slowly been erected in older civilizations." And even in 1931 (the Great Depression had surely challenged the American Dream in unprecedented ways), Adams laments the erosion of the values that had constituted the societal understanding of that dream: "We came to insist on business and money-making and material improvement as good in themselves [and to] consider an unthinking optimism essential, . . . regard[ing] criticism as obstructive and dangerous [and] think[ing] manners undemocratic, and a cultivated mind a hindrance to success, a sign of inefficient effeminacy . . . [S]ize and statistics of material development came to be more important in our eyes than quality and spiritual values." The eerie aptness of Adams's assessment, more than seventy years after it was written, suggests that the critique may be timeless; certainly Albee's indictment, expressed in *The American Dream,* written long after the Depression that was Adams's context, at the height of the prosperous late 1950s, seems unhappily relevant today.

Although many of the reviews of the premiere production were favorable, some were not; Albee has always had the ability to scandalize, and some critics were indeed scandalized. His preface (dated May 24, 1961) to the 1963 Signet edition of *The American Dream* acknowledges, gleefully, these negative reviews, accusing their authors of censorship and various other "misuse[s] of the critical function in American press letters." He writes that the "play is an examination of the American Scene, an attack on the substitution of artificial for real values in our society, a condemnation of complacency, cruelty, emasculation and vacuity. . . . it was my intention to offend—as well as amuse and entertain." And so he did, and would continue to do so for decades following.

Who's Afraid of Virginia Woolf?

This is Albee's most famous play—a fact he feels some mild resentment about: "It's nice to have a play everybody knows you for," he told *Playbill* in March 2005, "But everything you write shouldn't get compared to the popular one" (Wallenberg, 12). This echoes his comments in the Almeida Theatre's program for the London revival in 1996: "I find *Who's Afraid of Virginia Woolf?* hung about my neck like a shining medal of some sort—really nice but a trifle onerous . . . if there is a history years from now, and if I am a footnote in it, I daresay *Who's Afraid of Virginia Woolf?* will be the play identified with my name (or my name with it), and I, in my shallow grave, will not cavil much." It has had many major revivals since the first production in 1962, and with each pair of actors, these major roles change, as all great characters do when essayed by powerful actors and interpreted by intelligent directors.

The plot stands as one of the great theatrical treatments of the dysfunctional family, a subject American drama has been in love with from the beginning; this is not the drippy prime-time variety of television's version of "family drama" (more accurately, family "situation" whether the "sit" is "com" or not), but rather the obsessive reexamination of how families love and hate each other, the domestic battlefield where truth and illusion are locked in mortal combat.

Of course, it could be argued that dysfunctional families have always been drama's primary subject, long before the advent of realism with its devotion to psychology rather than philosophy; consider the *Oresteia* and *King Lear*.

Who's Afraid of Virginia Woolf? is not concerned only with domestic dysfunctionality. Albee's political and cultural agenda is woven into the characters' occupations; it follows, then, that this agenda is woven into the characters' preoccupations, and thus into the dialogue. Even George's and Martha's names—suggesting their surname may well be Washington—hint at a sociopolitical concern, and so they become representatives of both U.S. history (it is, after all, the college's History Department in which George is a "bog") and the moral values of the past. Their being childless suggests the end of all they represent culturally. Alan Schneider (the director who first gave American audiences both Albee and Beckett) referred to these characters as "dinosaurs battling on the cliff of emotional survival" (*American Theatre*, February 1986:6), implying both their enormous size and the noisy, high-stakes violence of their marriage. They are throwbacks, relics from a past when people married for love, unlike Nick and Honey, the couple of the future that Albee fears, who have married for money. For the younger couple, sterile self-interest and shameless ambition are the motivating forces that masquerade as their "family values." Nick, we learn, is an up-and-coming professor in the Biology Department ("the meat of things"), and George sees him as his enemy, both generationally and ideologically. Of course, in the nearly half century intervening since the play's composition, that future has become the present, and the manufacture and manipulation of life through what Martha calls "chromozones" is a fact and no longer merely a nightmarish possibility George fears.

In act 3, Martha listens to George's narrative about the moon's going down and then coming up again while he was "sailing past Majorca," and says, "That is not true! That is such a lie!" We do not know whether she is outraged about the moon or about Majorca. George replies, "You must not call everything a lie, Martha." And why not, we wonder; *is* there a truth? Nick's response is, "Hell, I don't know when you people are lying, or what," and Martha replies,

"You're damned right!" George echoes, "You're not supposed to" (1:283). This exchange distills two important ideas contained in the play. The first, the unavailability of a verifiable reality, is fundamental not only to Albee's work but central to most twentieth-century art. The second is self-reflexivity, the sly technique by which the play reminds us that it is a play—"lying" is inherent to the art form—while simultaneously engaging us in its realistic illusion.

Awareness of the precariousness of what we take for external reality extends back, in Western culture, to Plato's parable of the cave, which shows us that human beings inevitably take the evidence of our eyes as reality, when it is merely reality's shadow. This philosophical premise becomes a psychological premise, a way of explaining how entirely we are at the mercy of our individual points of view, and how difficult it is to separate our seeing from our need to see, our need to interpret life as we live it. In the twentieth century, this erosion of confidence in the soundness of reality was codified by the metaphoric value of great discoveries in physics: Einstein's general relativity, Heisenberg's uncertainty principle, and Bohr's theory of complementarity.

"Truth and illusion. Who knows the difference, eh, toots?" (1:284). Over and over George and Martha accuse each other of being unable to distinguish the facts from the fantasies of their lives, the most crucial of which is an imaginary child who has lived at the center of their marriage. Thus the title of act 3, "Exorcism," refers to the exorcism of that unreal son as well as of the demons of illusion that have overwhelmed their lives. The play's chief game is True or False, and in addition to the fake child and the elaborate narrative created around him from birth to death, there is the fake boxing match, the fake shotgun, the fake nursery rhymes, and Honey's fake pregnancy. The interpretive problem arises: is Albee showing us that when reality is too awful to bear we retreat into fantasy? Or is he showing us that when fantasy and reality are not kept distinct, despair is the inevitable outcome?

True or False is a game central to the theatrical enterprise: "Truth or illusion" governs not only the content of this play but of playmaking itself: any naturalistic play depends on our accepting its illu-

sion as reality (and thus we are engaged emotionally) while maintaining our consciousness of it as theater (and thus we are engaged
aesthetically). Drama asks us to be able to weep for a character and
simultaneously admire the actor's ability to make us weep, knowing
as we do that the evening's revelations will be new again tomorrow
night for a new audience, and Hamlet will die again.

Who's Afraid of Virginia Woolf? begins with a self-reflexive joke.
George and Martha noisily, drunkenly enter their house late at night,
we're told in the opening stage directions: "Set in darkness. Crash
against front door. MARTHA's laughter heard. Front door opens, lights
are switched on." To use the theatrical necessity of turning on the
lights to begin a play in the service of realism is to wink at the audience, reminding us that we are watching a play while simultaneously
creating the realistic illusion of people coming home late at night.
Having been, as Martha would say, "wunk" at by the production, we
are then invited in on the next theatrical joke as the actress playing
Martha plays Bette Davis: "What a dump. Hey, what's that from?
'What a dump!'" She goes on to describe the 1949 movie Beyond the
Forest, and repeats her imitation of Bette Davis's much-imitated
voice, complete with the requisite cigarette gesture. This is even funnier if we are watching a famous actress imitate a famous actress; the
list of famous Marthas is prodigious (a brief selection: Uta Hagen,
Elizabeth Taylor, Colleen Dewhurst, Diana Rigg, and, most recently
on Broadway, Kathleen Turner), and it would have been still funnier
if Albee had had his way when the film version was cast, and instead
of choosing Elizabeth Taylor, Ernest Lehman (the film's screenwriter
and producer) had used Bette Davis,who would have then been imitating herself.

During one of his talks in Valdez, Alaska (June 2002), where for
thirteen years Albee annually oversaw the Last Frontier Theatre
Conference, a member of the audience asked him to "reminisce"
about his experience of having Who's Afraid of Virginia Woolf?
adapted to the screen. Albee replied, "Will I reminisce? Will I rant?"
He explained that the original intention was to pair Bette Davis with
James Mason, and that Elizabeth Taylor and Richard Burton were the
wrong ages. (In fact, since Taylor was only thirty-three at the time,

Who's Afraid of Virginia Woolf? with Kathleen Turner and Bill Irwin, New York, 2005. (Photograph by T. Carol Rosegg.)

their son's birthday was changed from twenty-one, as it is in the play, to sixteen for the film.) When Albee saw the rough cut, he was "puzzled that the movie was in black and white, because I remembered having written the play in color." This raises intriguing questions about the conventions of realism and our assumption (from newspapers? old documentary newsreels?) that black-and-white film looks "realer" and, further, that "realer" is desirable for this play. And, once the underscoring was added, Albee felt that the play's conclusion had been compromised; the final scene, which should be "deeply sad, deeply ambiguous," became more optimistic with the addition of "movie music." (The film's conclusion is made additionally optimistic, even sentimental, by the camera's showing us the wedding ring on Burton's hand as it rests on Taylor's shoulder.) Albee added that, unlike *Virginia Woolf*, the film of *A Delicate Balance* had no screenplay. He was, finally, pleased to say that both films were rehearsed for weeks as stage plays before being filmed, and that both were shot in sequence. They are, he concluded, "both honorable films."

Names are a rich and intriguing aspect of the play. When Martha announces to George that they are expecting guests, and George, flabbergasted, asks, *"Who's* coming over?" the following dialogue ensues:

> MARTHA. What's-their-name.
> GEORGE. Who?
> MARTHA. WHAT'S-THEIR-NAME!
> GEORGE. Who what's-their-name?
> MARTHA. I don't know what their name is, George. (1:159)

They never do find out their guests' names, nor do Nick and Honey seem to know George's and Martha's, since Nick keeps calling George "Sir" and calls Martha "Lady" near the end. It is never clear whether Honey's name is actually Honey or whether that is simply Nick's habitual term of endearment. She never addresses Nick by name, but only as "Dear." Significantly, George and Martha always call each other by name: these people are individual personalities, not types.

Each of the three acts has its own title—an unusual feature in a play—and each title is informative: The first is "Fun and Games," and we will learn that all the vicious gambits are "oh-so-sad games" that also acquire names: Humiliate the Host, Get the Guests, Snap the Dragon, Hump the Hostess, Peel the Label, and, finally, Bringing Up Baby. Act 2 is called "Walpurgisnacht," the "Witches' Sabbath." This feast day, a celebration of wild and dangerous spirits, occurs in Goethe's play *Faust* and in Gounoud's opera of the same name, and Berlioz includes a Walpurgis Night in *Symphonie Fantastique.* Most interesting for our purposes here, the *Dies Irae*, the prayer for the dead, is almost always used in any musical representation of a Walpurgisnacht. It is the *Dies Irae* George intones in act 3 during Martha's "recitation" of their son's birth and childhood. Act 3 is aptly named "The Exorcism," the final purging of the demons—as well as the purging of the consolatory illusions—which have controlled their lives. George is the self-appointed exorcist, freeing everyone of evil spirits. Nick and Honey's marriage may not survive the exorcism; Albee commented to *Playbill* on the occasion of the 2005 revival, "As you begin the play, you have Honey and Nick, this very sweet, young married couple coming into a den of wolves. But by the end, you realize it's George and Martha's marriage that really means something and that it's very likely that Nick and Honey are finished as a relationship" (Wallenberg, 10).

And there is the play's own odd name, a question that Albee saw scrawled on the wall of a Greenwich Village bar. The title both provides and withholds information about the play that follows it. Virginia Woolf, the twentieth-century novelist and high priestess of the inner life—her most famous novels are *Mrs. Dalloway, To the Lighthouse,* and *The Waves*—was, along with James Joyce, the creator of the modernist technique of stream-of-consciousness narrative. In Woolf's fiction, this technique becomes a means for the rigorous and elegant examination of a character's motives, self-delusions, and self-awareness. It is a method utterly dependent on intimacy between the reader and the character—an intimacy Albee develops between character and audience. Clearly identifying the play's population as "college types like us," as George sardonically calls them and himself, the title further assumes an audience who are also "college types," who will understand the literary reference. The parodic nursery rhyme (to the tune, presumably, of "Who's afraid of the big bad wolf") is a gauge of the tone of the party at the president's house and of this academic world's cocktail wit. That the title becomes a question to be answered in the final scene is telling: the tone has shaded from social cleverness to a profound moment of self-discovery and intimate revelation, as Martha answers George's singing of the jingle with "I . . . am . . . George . . . I . . . am" (1:311). George nods in response—in sympathy? in acknowledgment of her fear? in agreement and admission of his own fear?—and their ambiguous tableau concludes the play.

We, as "college types," are expected to understand other allusions as well; when George arrives in act 3 with his bouquet of snapdragons (continuing the motif of "snap" throughout their climactic arguing in act 2), he presents it saying, "Flores; flores para los meurtos" (i.e., "Flowers, flowers for the dead"), quoting from Tennessee Williams's *A Streetcar Named Desire,* and suggesting a vast analogy between the two plays, as well as Albee's tip of the hat to the great precedent. It is also and more obviously an anticipation of the "death" of their son, which George has already planned as his ultimate revenge and their liberation. Martha wittily switches theatrical allusion when she curtsies to accept his flowers and cries with mock delight, "Pansies! Rosemary! Violence! My wedding bouquet!" (1:281). This line is from *Kiss Me Kate,* although there the word is "violets"; we cannot fully get the joke if we do not hear the change and recognize that Martha's wedding bouquet has certainly included violence. *Kiss Me Kate* is, of course, the musical comedy based on Shakespeare's *The Taming of the Shrew,* and uses as its device the central couple battling onstage in their Shakespearean roles and offstage as themselves. (That Elizabeth Taylor and Richard Burton were so celebrated a battling married couple, and that they made a filmed version of *The Taming of the Shrew* the following year, adds amusing layers here.) Seeing Martha in this literary context, as the shrew who is tamed by the play's end, provokes interpretive possibilities, especially as *The Taming of the Shrew* has long vexed feminists and since gender dominance is so clearly an issue for both couples in *Who's Afraid of Virginia Woolf?*

Another allusion we are expected to think about is George's decision to read, at four o'clock in the morning, Spengler's *Decline of the West.* The passage he chooses is significant: "And the west, encumbered by crippling alliances, and burdened with a morality too rigid to accommodate itself to the swing of events, must . . . eventually . . . fall." This passage becomes even more powerful in the text as Albee revised it for the *Collected Plays,* where it now ends act 2. Earlier, after the game of Get the Guests ends with Honey in tears and Nick outraged—not on his wife's behalf but his own—George tells Nick, "Well, you just rearrange your alliances, boy. You just pick up the pieces where you can," the implication being that Nick will not be "encumbered by crippling alliances." Spengler's view of history examines the triumph of economic power over culture, the surrender of the values of the past and the consequential loss of humanism. Albee's political agenda is embedded in the play, since the university town that is the play's locale is "New Carthage," and if Martha is, by virtue of her position, the queen of New Carthage, she is the Dido to Nick's Aeneas, the "historical inevitability" whose new Rome represents the soulless, militarized world George fears:

> You take the trouble to construct a civilization . . . to . . . to build a society, based on the principles of . . . of principle . . . you endeavor to make communicable sense out of natural order, morality out of the unnatural disorder of man's mind . . . you make government and art, and realize that they are, must be, both the same . . . you bring things to the saddest of all points . . . to the point where there *is* something to lose . . . then all at once, through all the music, through all the sensible sounds of men building, attempting comes the *Dies Irae*. And what is it? What does the trumpet sound? Up yours. I suppose there's justice to it, after all the years . . . Up yours. (1:232)

Albee wrote a travel article in the *New York Times* about his recent trip to Easter Island, which he called the fulfillment of a longtime dream. He writes, "Way before the movie 'Planet of the Apes' showed us the Statue of Liberty half buried in the sand, I have felt the need to experience cultures which grew, fell into decadence and vanished. These are probably cautionary tales even beyond their aesthetic marvel" ("Easter Island," 1). The allure of "cautionary tales" informs *Who's Afraid of Virginia Woolf?* as it does all the plays in volume 1 of *The Collected Plays*.

One of those early plays, Albee's most overtly political work, *The Death of Bessie Smith* ends with an image of a blazing sunset, suggesting that a Western world of civilized values has gone down in flames. Later, in *Seascape*, Charlie attempts to explain evolution to the two giant lizards in this way:

> A hundred million years? Ten times that? Well, a distance certainly. . . . That heartbreaking second when it all got together, the sugars and the acids and the ultraviolets, and the next thing you knew there were tangerines and string quartets. (2:437)

Thus, George's prediction of the future seems to be the loss of what has been gained over eons, and we are returned once again to the lesson learned in *The Zoo Story*, "What is gained is loss."

Who's Afraid of Virginia Woolf? is also a play about drunks, as so many classic American plays are; perhaps the most prevalent stage business in twentieth-century American dramatic literature is the pouring of drinks. Although Nick says, "After a while you don't get any drunker, do you?" it is obvious that they do: many of the events of the play are triggered by the inebriation of four people who drank steadily at the party before the play begins and then continue at George and Martha's house from "after two o'clock in the morning" until near daybreak ("it will be dawn soon"), when the play ends. The three-hour running time, including the intermissions, matches the chronology of the action of the play; at the end of act 1, George is left alone on stage, which is where we find him, with some little time having elapsed—enough for Nick to have gone to check on Honey—at the start of act 2. Act 2 ends (in the revised version) with the sounds of laughter and breaking dishes in the kitchen, as Martha's sex play with Nick begins and George hurls his book, hitting the chimes and thus creating more sound effects, vowing, "I'm going to get you" (1:272). He exits, leaving the front door open. When act 3 begins, Martha enters after spending an intermission's worth of time in the bedroom with Nick, while George has been out picking flowers.

Impaired judgment and weakened social inhibitions are realistic effects of many hours of drinking, but they do not explain the dramatic donnée, Martha's invitation to their guests. The most obvious reason Martha invited them is that "Daddy said we should be nice to them," but she also finds Nick attractive; beyond these superficial motives, the invitation seems to be another desperate attempt to distract herself from the grim truths of her life alone with George. But why would two strangers stay so long, watch so much emotional mayhem, and tolerate so much abuse? (This question echoes the nagging question of *The Zoo Story:* why would Peter, a New Yorker, stay so long and listen to Jerry, a bizarre and dangerous stranger?) The careerist answer is that Nick is ambitious, and Martha is the daughter of the president of the college. The psychological answer is the equivalent of "gaper delay," the fascinated horror of watching a social situation turn grotesquely ugly. The theatrical answer is that what goes on during that evening is simply more interesting than anything else Nick and Honey might do alone. There is, further, some human impulse to truth-telling, the intoxication of stripping away comforting illusions; as George tells Honey, "We all peel labels, sweetie; and when you get through the skin, all three layers, through the muscle, slosh aside the organs [. . .] and get down to bone [. . .] When you get down to bone, you haven't got all the way, yet. There's something inside the bone . . . the marrow . . . and that's what you gotta get at." And get at it they do.

Albee revised *Who's Afraid of Virginia Woolf?* for the Broadway revival in 2005. In addition to easy changes that reflect the times (i.e., "Screw you" becomes "Fuck you" and "Mother" becomes "Mother-fucker"), Albee made significant alterations. The first major cut is a major improvement:

Early on, in the original act 1, as Nick and Honey arrive, ringing the doorbell, but before they enter, George warns Martha; what follows has been entirely omitted from the new version):

GEORGE. *(Moves a little toward the door, smiling slightly)* All right, love . . . whatever love wants. *(Stops)* Just don't start on the bit, that's all.

MARTHA. The bit? The bit? What kind of language is that? What are you talking about?

GEORGE. The bit. Just don't start in on the bit.

MARTHA. You imitating one of your students, for God's sake? What are you trying to do? WHAT BIT?

GEORGE. Just don't start in on the bit about the kid, that's all.

MARTHA. What do you take me for?

GEORGE. Much too much.

MARTHA. *(Really angered)* Yeah? Well, I'll start on the kid if I want to.

GEORGE. Just leave the kid out of this.

MARTHA. *(Threatening)* He's mine as much as he is yours. I'll talk about him if I want to.

GEORGE. I'd advise against it, Martha.

MARTHA. Well, good for you. *(Knock)* C'mon in. Get over there and open the door!

GEORGE. You've been advised.
MARTHA. Yeah . . . sure. Get over there! (Signet ed., 18–19)

The follow-up deletion comes slightly later in the act 1 when George warns Martha again, "Just don't shoot your mouth off . . . about . . . you-know-what."

Martha replies, "*(Surprisingly vehement)* I'll talk about any goddamn thing I want to, George!" Martha's "C'mon" to Honey, with the line that precedes it, "Any goddam thing I want to!" has also been dropped (Signet ed., 29–30).

This dialogue always seemed both puzzling and dramatically self-defeating; if the enormous decision to end the mutual pretense of an imaginary child rests on Martha's having finally revealed their secret to Honey, why would George refer to this revelation as a "bit," which suggests that her indiscretion happens with some regularity? Near the end of the play, Martha asks George why he had to kill the child, and he replies, "You broke our rule, baby. You mentioned him to someone else" (1:307). Martha achingly describes how hard it has been for her to keep their secret ("Sometimes when it's late, and . . . and everybody else is . . . talking . . . I forget and I . . . want to mention him . . . but I HOLD ON . . . I hold on . . . but I've wanted to . . . so often . . . oh George," 1:308); this declaration is not possible if the betrayal is merely a "bit," nor is the betrayal a betrayal if it has happened repeatedly in the past. As the shocking truth finally dawns on Nick ("Jesus Christ, I think I understand this"), we should have had the same shock (although we understand before Nick does), which is not possible if we have already heard the now-omitted exchange. Thus the new version of the script is greatly improved by the excision of this cumbersome and misleading dialogue.

In act 2, after the game of Get the Guests, Albee has moved lines from the end (Signet ed., 177) of the act to the middle. George addresses Honey: "How do you do it? Hunh? How do you make your secret little murders studboy doesn't know about, hunh? Pills? PILLS? You got a secret supply of pills? Or what? Apple jelly? WILL POWER?" (1:254).

Several significant cuts in act 3, involving Honey's unwitting involvement in George's last game, strike me as damaging. When George tells Martha about the arrival of a telegram, in the original script, George's line, "Martha . . . I can hardly bring myself to say it" is interrupted by Honey's "Don't."

> GEORGE. *(to HONEY)* Do you want to do it?
> HONEY. *(defending herself against an attack of bees)* No no no no no.
> (Signet ed., 230)

George's manipulation of Honey's seeming complicity in his last game continues later in the scene. After George has told Martha he cannot show her the telegram because he "ate it" and after she spits in his face and Nick chastises George for "making an ugly godddam joke like that" at "a time like this," George turns to Honey, demanding verification:

> GEORGE. *(Snapping his fingers at HONEY)* Did I eat the telegram or did I not?
> HONEY. Yes, yes you ate it. I watched . . . I watched you . . . you . . . you ate it all down.
> GEORGE. *(Prompting)* . . . like a good boy.
> HONEY. . . . like a . . . g-g-good . . . boy. Yes. (Signet ed., 234–35)

This cut eliminates a layer of complexity in the game that reveals George's ruthlessness (Honey has suffered greatly at his hands), as well as eliminating a layer of comedy. This horrifying moment, with Honey's childish/maternal locution ("you ate it all down") is employed in the destruction of the couple's most cherished illusion. The cut also eliminates from the new version this crucial example of the issue most central to the play, "truth or illusion."

Bill Irwin was a high-profile George in the Broadway revival of 2005 and the national tour in 2007, and his understanding of the play is interesting: "Even though none of the characters on stage have children, this is a play about parenthood, about the fierce drive within us to be parents and what that can do to us" ("Interview with Ida Goldberg," 20). Irwin told an interviewer in *pmny* that Albee had warned him about how demanding the role is: "Once you've played

George in my play no other role with the possible exception of Hamlet will challenge you quite as much as far as magnitude of text, complexity of language and the challenge of working on many planes at the same time."

The role's allure also captured Patrick Stewart; after playing George for only four weeks in 1987, he has been longing to reprise it ever since:

> I felt I had taken possession of the play as it had taken possession of me. . . . It is a very, very great play, I think it is one of the great plays of the 20th century, a masterpiece of modern American theatre. And there is not a day goes by when I don't think about it. . . . Albee is astonishingly brilliant. . . . He can write in a way which is tragic and wonderfully funny at the same time—extraordinary. (Stewart, 68)

As Martha says of the long-ago boxing match, "It was awful, really. It was funny, but it was awful" (1:191).

Tiny Alice

In *The Goat* there is a buried joke for Albee aficionados; the central character, Martin, is reminiscing with his old friend Ross about their womanizing college days:

> ROSS. *(Trying to recall)* What were their names?
> MARTIN. Mine was Alice.
> ROSS. Big girl.
> MARTIN. Large Alice.
> ROSS. Right! Mine was Trudy, or Trixie, or . . . (3:562–63)

It takes a second, but then Martin's line, "Large Alice" gets a laugh from everyone in the audience who knows Albee wrote a play called *Tiny Alice.*

A notorious flop nearly forty years ago, *Tiny Alice* came roaring back in a gorgeous New York revival directed by Mark Lamos in 2000, featuring Richard Thomas as Brother Julian, the sacrificial lamb who is preyed upon by a wolfish Lawyer, a disaffected Butler, a pompous Cardinal, and an alabaster temptress called Miss Alice.

The play is a peculiar combination of passionate arias on religious martyrdom and boulevard exchanges of sophisticated cynicism; its power lies in its intensity and elusiveness, its unexpected wit and immense style, skirting the pretentious and portentous. As Albee summed it up: *Tiny Alice* is "a perfectly straightforward metaphysical melodrama having to do with the relationship of faith to sexual hysteria and the nonexistence of a god created by man in his own image." This somewhat arch sarcasm—the remark has been much-quoted and reappears in his introduction to volume 1 of *The Collected Plays* (1:8)—reflects Albee's exasperation with the initial critical bafflement. In retrospect, the similarities between *Tiny Alice* and his other plays are stronger than the differences: philosophically, *Tiny Alice* is a meditation on the theme of illusion and reality; stylistically, *Tiny Alice* showcases Albee's characteristic way of expressing immense ideas in witty dialogue; thematically, *Tiny Alice* develops, by metaphoric extension, the larger implications of sexual temptation and betrayal—of oneself and by oneself.

The plot of *Tiny Alice* is difficult to summarize, and for this very reason it is necessary to try.

A Lawyer, functioning as an emissary from a fabulously rich woman, offers the Cardinal one billion dollars each year for twenty years (this is a revision for the *Collected Plays* from the original one hundred million in 1964) in exchange for Julian, a lay brother who is the Cardinal's secretary. Initially, Julian seems to be merely a go-between who will iron out the details of the "grant." Soon after his first visit, however, he is asked to move into her castle, and eventually, after his discovery of the pleasures of the extraordinary wine cellar and the exhilarations of horseback riding, he rediscovers his sexuality and marries the seductive Miss Alice.

The six years that are blank on Brother Julian's curriculum vitae were, we learn, spent in a "mental home"; he committed himself when he felt his faith "depart," and during that time he was subject to experiences that may or may not have been hallucinations, the most vivid and troubling of which was a sexual liaison with a patient who thought she was the Virgin Mary. "My faith and my sanity . . . they are one and the same" (1:453). This woman, like Miss Alice (whose lovers include both the Lawyer and the Butler), furthers Albee's comment on the spiritualizing of sexuality and the sexualizing of spirituality; Julian's longing for religious ecstasy is linked to his longing for sexual ecstasy. Albee's plays are soaked in sex, and

Tiny Alice, with Richard Thomas and Laila Roberts, Second Stage Theatre, New York, 2000. (Photograph by T. Charles Erickson.)

even in this play, so far removed from his many marriage plays, sexuality is the lens through which he looks at life.

Brother Julian's religious struggle, and the reason he refused ordination as a priest although he had accepted the stricture of chastity, was based in a profound objection to the literalization of God, the reductive impulse of organized religion that diminishes the abstract into the easily understood, a failure of the theological imagination. "Men create a false God in their own image, it is easier for them!" (1:452). He is troubled by "the chasm between the nature of God and the uses to which men put . . . God" (1:452).

It is thus deeply ironic that Brother Julian is ultimately martyred to such "uses" and to a belief system he finds simplistic. The Cardinal, in effect, sells him, revealing the corruption of the church, while the triumvirate of the Lawyer, the Butler, and Miss Alice, all seemingly creatures of the world, are devotees in service of a God who demands human sacrifice. This sacrifice is required both to sustain the faith and to eliminate a man who doubts the need for such sacrifices to a literalized God. Once Julian is "theirs," and the wedding has taken place, they shoot him, leaving him to bleed to death on the floor while he contemplates the symbolic absurdity of a phrenological head with Miss Alice's wig on it: the emblem of a God made in our image, the quasi-scientific merged with the quasi-human, the cosmic joke brought grotesquely home. Suggestions of Job in Brother Julian's cry, "SHOW THYSELF! I DEMAND THEE!" (1:547) mingle with suggestions of Jesus, as he dies in the posture Albee specifies in the stage directions: "arms wide, should resemble a crucifixion." Thus Brother Julian becomes the Christ figure, crying out, at the end, "Alice? ALICE? MY GOD, WHY HAST THOU FORSAKEN ME?" (1:548). Whether this constitutes a deathbed conversion or an ironic comment on the ludicrous upshot of his noble struggle lingers as an ambiguity, just as the New Testament's Gospels offer irresolvable inconsistencies: according to both Matthew and Mark, Christ's final words were "My God, my God, why hast thou forsaken me?" but according to Luke, Christ's last words were "Father into thy hands I commend my spirit." According to John, the last line is "It is finished."

Julian describes the sadness he felt at the beginning of his hallucinating episodes,: "I am going from myself again. How very, very sad . . . everything. Loss, great loss." What Jerry learned in *The Zoo Story* is that "what is gained is loss." What loss has Julian gained? The loss of innocence? hope? sanity? insanity? faith? the illusion of love? Is his sacrifice really suicide? Has he, by this crucifixion, fulfilled his deepest longing for martyrdom? He tells Miss Alice, "I have . . . dreamed of sacrifice" (1:507). Is this, then, a perversely happy ending? Or is the real gain the loss of meaning:

> JULIAN. What does it mean if the pain . . . ebbs?
> BUTLER. It means the agony is less. (1:542)

The apparent servant to the others, the Butler, may be in charge after all. During Julian's agony, he checks the room: "All in order, I think

[. . .] . My work done" (1:545). He then kisses Julian on the forehead, the Judas kiss. Thus, perhaps, the solution to the mystery: the Butler did it.

The castle, in which most of the action takes place, and in which all the characters but the Cardinal live, contains within its gigantic stone walls a tiny model of itself. (This is a set designer's heaven: Albee's directions require that it be a "huge doll's-house model of the building of which the present room is a part." He suggests a minimum of twelve feet long and proportionately high.) Brother Julian marvels at this creation when he first arrives, and is astounded when he looks through its little windows to see that every room is completely furnished, with every detail replicated. There is even a tinier castle inside the model, in exactly the location of the one he is looking into. The play's title becomes the key to the play's secret and the way we understand Julian's dying words: Alice, Tiny Alice, who dwells within the tiny model of the castle, is God; "Miss Alice" is merely her surrogate, her priest, her instrument.

In act 1, scene 2, so early in the play that we might not grasp its importance, the Butler gives us our first clue as to the model's symbolic implications: "That someone would . . . well, for heaven's sake, that someone would build . . . *(Refers to the set)* . . . *this* . . . castle? . . . and then . . . duplicate it in such a precise miniature, so exactly" (1:438). His apparently naturalistic interjection, "for heaven's sake," is crucial here: it could be literal (i.e., in devotion to God), or it could suggest the Platonic idea that everything earthly is a knockoff of the ideal that exists on some other plane. To consider that the larger, the assumedly "real" castle is the imitation and that the model is the true castle in which Tiny Alice exists, is to challenge not only the notion of reality but the human idea of proportion (i.e., that big equals powerful and that the gauge of the universe is anthropomorphic). "It's remarkable craftsmanship, though. Remarkable" (1:439). Who is the craftsman? Is this God's handiwork—creating a world for people to live in? Or man's handiwork—creating an image to worship? (One is reminded here of the joke Beckett used in *Endgame:* A man, exasperated with his tailor for taking so long to make a pair of trousers, finally explodes with "God damn you to hell, Sir, no, it's indecent, there are limits! In six days, do you hear me, in six days, God made the world. Yes Sir, no less, Sir, the WORLD! And you are not bloody capable of making me a pair of trousers in three months!" To which the tailor replies, "But my dear Sir, my dear Sir, look—at the world—and look at my TROUSERS!")

It is also worth noting that although Albee has focused on the Roman Catholic Church, Miss Alice makes grants to "the Protestants as well, the Jews . . . hospitals, universities, orchestras, revolutions here and there" (1:432). The implication seems to be that all cultural and societal institutions are corrupt and greedy, and that Alice's appetite for human sacrifice, in whatever name, is insatiable, since that is the way she sustains herself. Albee thus implies that any organization, cause, religion, or cult convinces itself of its nobility, justness, and truth by exchanging death and blood for "loot." Thus Albee's disgust with and condemnation of our world is far-reaching and vitriolic.

Consider, too, the almost inescapable allusion to Kafka's *The Castle*, his last and unfinished work; that novel is deeply concerned with the religious dichotomy between the true way and our notion of the true way. The central character "K," who is a land surveyor, is summoned to the Castle, but once he arrives in the village (i.e., Prague) it becomes clear his work is not needed. He is repeatedly denied access both to the mysterious authorities who summoned him and the society in which he dwells. He is, like Julian, "poised" (a word of great significance in *A Delicate Balance*) between worlds, neither of which he feels fully a part of. The allegory extends beyond social alienation to the modernist theme of cosmic alienation. Kafka's work is always allegorical; Albee's work is often allegorical, as it is in *Tiny Alice*.

The play's multivalence grows if we add a theatrical interpretation to the theological interpretation. The audience is looking at a set—a model, as all sets are, of the "reality" the playwright wishes to represent or evoke; this is true however surreal, unreal, nonreal the play's world is. Albee, the god of this creation, has dreamed up and directed someone to build the castle and, likewise, the model within it, and within that model, although we cannot see the ever-diminishing models within, we take *on faith* their presence. Because drama holds a mirror up to nature, because its task is to reveal ourselves to ourselves, the very act of building a set holds up a mirror, a symbolic act in our built world. Thus, Tiny Alice may represent the playwright, the God who pares his fingernails behind his creation, as Joyce put it. Read this way, the play acquires another layer of meaning: Brother Julian is martyred to the Artist whose creation Julian inhabits: a character is always born of and sacrificed to the playwright's necessity, just as the actor's identity is sacrificed to his character's. Plot also exacts its sacrifice. The Lawyer brutally bullies Miss Alice: "Don't you dare mess this thing up. You behave the way I've told you; you PLAY ACT. You do your part; STRAIGHT" (1:475). The implication is that no devout follower ever lives fully within the confines of the demands of his faith, just as no actor every lives fully within the confines of his role. Playacting is part of "doing your part." When, after the fire in the chapel, Miss Alice seems relieved that it has not been apocalyptic, that "we are not . . . consumed," Julian asks, "Is there anything to be frightened of, Miss Alice?" She replies, after a long pause, "Always" (1:488). The characters in *A Delicate Balance* know this to be true as well; no one is immune to "the terror."

That "all the world's a stage" is certainly not news, but the idea does become especially layered here: When we first meet Miss Alice, she appears to be a "withered crone, her hair gray and white and matted, she is bent, she moves with two canes" and she speaks in a "cracked and ancient voice" (1:454). We soon discover that she is acting—she straightens up, drops the canes, speaks in a youthful voice, removes her wig (later to reappear on the phrenological head), and removes her mask, revealing the Miss Alice within the Miss Alice. (There is a meaningful joke—or fact—later on when Julian describes his periods of hallucination, and Miss Alice replies, "There was no feeling of terror in this? I would be *beside myself*" [1:463; emphasis added]). That Julian mistakenly thinks (as does the audience) after open-mouthed amazement, that this young, beautiful woman is the "real" Miss Alice, is one of the problems the play offers and one of the ongoing facts of theater: the person we are looking at is never the character that person represents. The immense metaphor theater provides is "the idea of the thing, and not the thing itself," as Wallace Stevens put it. As the Lawyer tells Julian early on, "Never confuse the representative of a . . . thing with the thing itself" (1:449). Not only does this apply to the Alice/Alice problem, the God/Christ problem, the God/church problem, but also to the play/production problem (the playwright's idea as manifested onstage), not to mention the text/interpretation problem (amply demonstrated here).

The "Loathly Lady" tale is a convention of medieval literature and revolves around a test of a young man's (sometimes a knight's) mettle: in his quest to find the answer to the question, "What do women desire?" (*pace* Freud), he meets an ancient, ugly woman, the Loathly Lady, who offers him the answer in exchange for his marrying her. He agrees, but is too repulsed to sleep with her. She then offers him options: she can be ugly by day and beautiful by night or vice versa. He finds neither a happy alternative, and tells her to do whatever she wants. *That* of course is the right answer, since what women want is what Chaucer's Wife of Bath (her tale is Chaucer's version of the Loathly Lady story) calls "maistrie." The young man's reward is the transformation of the old hag into a young and beautiful wife. In the Gawain versions of the story in the Arthurian legends, the lady has been under a spell that the knight's "courtesy" has broken. The interpretive possibilities for *Tiny Alice* are many and tempting.

Another layer of meaning emerges if we consider literature's most famous Alice, the one in Wonderland, suggesting the bizarre multidimensions of "reality" and our fall from innocence as wishes are fulfilled. If we consider the literary history of Lewis Carroll's *Alice in Wonderland* and *Alice's Adventures Underground,* we see that the "real" person, clergyman-mathematician Charles Lutwidge Dodgson, has vanished in time, while the "imaginary" person, tiny Carroll, endures.

If we shift interpretation to the psychological arena, it is possible to consider the play a staging of Julian's mind wherein each character represents an aspect of his being, and the play's struggle is an internal one made manifest—an externalizing of a conflict that is often a tantalizing option in an Albee play (cf. *The Zoo Story, Seascape*). If crises—spiritual or sexual or philosophical—are always threatening to disintegrate the personality, perhaps Brother Julian's destruction by the other three characters is emblematic of his loss of faith: the pressures exerted by the world have crushed him, and thus, metaphorically, the delicate balance of his soul has tipped irrevocably. If the dark night of the soul ends not in revelation but in crucifixion, the quest—for God, for purity, for goodness, for truth—is over, and the forces of corruption triumph. Welcome to the world, Julian. As Miss Alice tells him, "Every monster was a man first, Julian; every dictator was a colonel who vowed to retire once the revolution was done" (1:504). In a perfectly Beckettian line, Julian cries out, "I have not accepted *half*, for nothing" (1:534).

What Julian's final act of acceptance means is highly ambiguous. In the last moments of his life—and of the play—"A great shadow, or darkening, fills the stage, it is the shadow of a great presence filling the room. The area on Julian and around him stays in some light, but, for the rest, it is as if ink were moving through paper. . . . The sounds [breathing and heartbeats] become enormous," and we hear the last "thump thump thump thump thump thump" while the lights on Julian fade slowly to black. Does this final stage image show us the death of the body, or the death of the soul, or the end of the internal struggle, or Huge Alice looming over the world of *Tiny Alice*, suggesting that the play exists only within a model, and that the big castle is merely another tiny castle within some larger castle? In any event, darkness and silence swallow up the character, and, as they must in any theatrical event, darkness and silence swallow up the play.

A Delicate Balance

The phrase *a delicate balance* appears in spoken and written English in contexts as varied as global politics and ecology, chronic illness and civil liberties, cloud clusters and credit management. It always implies a fragile precariousness, where the slightest pressure might tip the delicately balanced parts; the general assumption is that it is important and desirable to maintain the balance. This is not Albee's meaning; in this long, elegant play, the balance is, indeed, maintained—familial, psychological, social—but at such cost that its desirability is ironically undermined. Albee's plays frequently review the hazards of security, the damage that valuing safety can do to life, and the play's resolution—the restoration of balance—which would, in a conventional play, provide a happy ending is, here, a defeat. The only solace for these characters lies in dishonesty, and Albee will not permit the astute audience to fully participate in the characters' self-deceit, even as we recognize it may be our own. It is interesting to contrast this with the earlier three-act play about marriage, *Who's Afraid of Virginia Woolf?* where the balance is tipped and real growth is, if not achieved, at least posited as possible at the end. That ending, the promise of dawn and a metaphorical as well as a literal new day, is ironically echoed in *A Delicate Balance,* where, after another long and tormented night, the characters greet the new day with early morning drinks, and, after the departure of Harry and Edna, Agnes concludes, "Well, they're *safely* [emphasis added] gone . . . and we'll all forget . . . quite soon. *(Pause)* Come now; we can begin the day" (2:122).

Psychological balance is the subject of the play's opening as Agnes archly contemplates the possibility of "going quite mad," which she speaks of as "a drifting"; she imagines this would not be unpleasant but for "the only outweighing thing"—that it would make her "a stranger in . . . the world, quite . . . uninvolved" (2:19). Her word "outweighing" is interesting, as it appears in the first moments of a play with *balance* in the title; the irony to be revealed in the course of the three acts that follow this speech suggest her "involvement" is already minimal, and that genuine involvement would very definitely tip the delicate balancing act that is her life. Her final speech, creating a perfect loop of the play's structure, echoes her first: "What I find most astonishing—aside from my belief that I will, one day . . . lose my mind—but when? Never, I begin to think, as the years go by [. . .]" (2:122). The play has "gone by" and she has not, in fact, lost her mind, despite provocation. Her sanity is, as she sees it, crucial to the ongoing, delicately balanced life of the family: "I am the one member of this . . . reasonably happy family blessed and burdened with the ability to view a situation objectively while I'm in it. [. . .] There is a balance to be maintained, after all, though the rest of you teeter, unconcerned or uncaring, *assuming* you're on level ground [. . .] And I must be the fulcrum" (2:67). The sentence structure and thus the rhythm of her speech is remarkable for its balance.

The life she lives is committed to safely maintaining the equilibrium, not only of her sanity but of her very identity: "Well, you know how little I vary; goodness, I can't even raise my voice excepting the most calamitous of events, and I find that both joy and sorrow work their . . . wonders in me more . . . evenly, slowly, with*in*, than most; a suntan rather than a scalding. There are no mountains in my life . . . nor chasms. It is a rolling, pleasant land . . . verdant, my darling, thank you" (2:23). Forty years later Albee would have Peter in "Homelife" remind his wife of their similar marital contract: "calm seas and prosperous voyage."

Moral balance is the subject of Tobias's self-revelatory speech in act 1; the beleaguered husband of the household tells his wife Agnes and sister-in-law Claire about a cat he had when he was a young man. It was an old cat, one he had owned since childhood, and one day he realized the cat "didn't like me anymore." The cat resists all his overtures, all his attempts to force a return to earlier affection, until finally, rejected, he discovers, "I *hated* her! [. . .] She and I had lived together and been, well, you know, friends, and . . . there was no *reason*. And I hated her for that. I hated her, well, I suppose because I was being accused of something, of . . . failing. [. . .] I resented . . . being judged. Being *betrayed*" (2:39). He has a veterinarian kill her. It is a painful speech, not only for its poignant content but for the rawness of its self-condemnation, like the dog story in *The Zoo Story*. Albee told his biographer, Mel Gussow: "It [the play] needed something a little bit Chekhovian and metaphorical [. . .] I wrote it [the cat story] rather quickly, and after I had written it I became aware that it was sort of a metaphor for the whole play rather than simply a specific thing in Tobias's life" (*ASJ*, 264). Both of these elements, the Chekhovian and the metaphorical, deserve discussion since they extend beyond Tobias's speech to the entire play.

The Chekhovian elements of *A Delicate Balance* include, most obviously, the large house that is filled, in the course of three acts, with various family members and friends, and then, at the end, emptied of them again. As each new person arrives, lingering tensions, longings, and disappointments surface, until the air is fairly humming with danger and exasperation. There are, too, those many articulate Chekhovian characters—some self-important, some self-denigrating, all capable of insight, albeit only partial, into their own preposterous and pitiable situations. They are recognizable types from the Chekhovian ensemble: the ineffectual men who are heads of households, given to denial or self-loathing, the grown daughters living lives of incomplete womanhood, the hangers-on who are entertaining drunks, the family friends whose sense of entitlement derives primarily from years shared.

Like Chekhov's families, this Albee family has a dependent, pathetic grown daughter, back home again—and it is worth noting that American drama is filled with adult unmarried children living at home (*Long Day's Journey Into Night* and *Death of a Salesman* for obvious examples). Of course Julia is not exactly unmarried, but rather much-married and much-divorced, a thirty-something whose adolescence is grotesquely protracted. Julia's gun-waving tantrum is similar to the one in *Uncle Vanya* (Chekhov's famous injunction: a gun on the wall in the beginning needs to go off by the end), doing no real damage, thus exposing the ineffectuality of the gun-waver and the crucial fact that for both Chekhov and Albee, the drama lies elsewhere.

The challenge of change—the necessity of it and the impossibility of it—is the engine that drives Chekhov's masterworks, *Uncle Vanya, Three Sisters,* and *The Cherry Orchard,* and the same engine drives *A Delicate Balance.* The characters are so brave and so weak that the reader's or audience's response is often a Chekhovian combination of amusement, sympathy, and irritation. Finally, sadly, we forgive Albee's characters as we forgive Chekhov's, as we ruefully forgive ourselves. Albee's title might well apply, descriptively, to any Chekhov play: the flimsy accommodations are, in the progress of Chekhov's plays, as they are here, nearly wrecked, and the balance is restored at great cost. This is reflected in the play's conventional structure; the balance that is delineated and revealed to be very tenuous in act 1 is radically disrupted in act 2 and finally restored in act 3. The restoration of order is both a relief and a capitulation; the bittersweet resolutions of Chekhov's plays are echoed in *A Delicate Balance* in the brave pathos of soldiering on.

Metaphorically, Tobias's cat story is about, first, inexplicable emotional betrayal, followed by revenge, followed by guilt. It is this guilt—Tobias's abiding remorse for having succumbed to his worst feelings, his lowest nature, and the consequent need to atone—that motivates his need to succor his friends, Harry and Edna. In the middle of Tobias's "aria" near the end of the play, the stage directions read: "It must have in its performance all the horror and exuberance of a man who has kept his emotions under control too long" (2:114). These directions explain the surprisingly passionate delivery, but do not explain the content:

> TOBIAS. yes! of course! I want you here! this is my house! i want you
> in it! i want your plague! you've got some terror with you? bring
> it in! [. . .] we've known each other all these years and we love
> each other don't we? DON'T WE LOVE EACH OTHER? [. . .] I like you
> Harry, yes, I really do, I don't like Edna but that's not half the
> point, I like you fine; I find my liking you has limits . . . BUT
> THOSE ARE MY LIMITS! NOT YOURS! [. . .] YOU BRING YOUR TERROR
> AND YOU COME IN HERE AND YOU LIVE WITH US! YOU BRING YOUR
> PLAGUE! YOU STAY WITH US! I DON'T WANT YOU HERE! I DON'T
> LOVE YOU! BUT BY GOD . . . YOU STAY!! (2:115–17)

The story of the cat provides the emotional elucidation of this spectacular speech. He tries, all these years later, to understand the lingering power of the cat event in his life: "She and I had lived together and had been, well, you know, friends, and . . . there was no *reason*. And I hated her for that. I hated her, well, I suppose because I was being accused of something of . . . failing" (2:39). So, too, he has been "friends" for forty years with Harry and Edna, and it becomes vital to him not to fail them as he failed the cat. But with the life-ironies Albee especially relishes, it is Harry and Edna's failure—to accept his offer of friendship, of help, of shelter from the metaphysical storm— that ends the play.

The cat story also elucidates Tobias's character: having discovered early on his capacity for hatred and revenge, he has become a decorous, sympathetic, and utterly civilized man, keeping his emotional life under genteel wraps lest the man he glimpsed himself to be ever reappear. Tobias is like Peter in "Homelife," sharing his habitual restraint. Peter has been so thoughtful and tame a lover that his wife wishes he were otherwise, and he finally tells her about the violent sexual experience he had in college, after which he vowed never to be so carried away again. Tobias's sexual history is similarly revealed; Agnes remembers that after their son died, Tobias's love-making changed, and despite Agnes's pleading, his unstated refusal to risk having another child, to risk another loss, produced "such . . . silent . . . sad, disgusted . . . love" (2:101). Both men, like so many other Albee characters, illustrate what Albee sees as the dangers of safety.

The one character in the play who has seemingly eschewed safety is Claire, Agnes's alcoholic sister. Unrepentant and unrestrained, she behaves badly whenever she pleases, although her attitude of *épater le bourgeois* grows tedious in its protracted adolescence. We learn, by implication at least, that, years before, she had sexual flings with both Harry and Tobias. She seems to be the only person in the family who has a real sense of humor and who is capable of genuine warmth. She rightly tells Julia that her need for the safety of home is self-destructive:

> CLAIRE. But you've come back home, haven't you? And didn't you—with the others?
> JULIA. Where else am I supposed to go?
> CLAIRE. It's a great big world, baby. There are hotels, new cities. Home is the quickest road to Reno I know of. (2:61)

Julia retaliates accurately: "You've had a lot of experience in these matters, Claire," ironically pointing up that she is the only one in the play who has not been married, and Claire self-ironizes in her reply to Julia: "Sidelines! Good seats, right on the fifty-yard line, objective observer" (2:61); as Agnes has noted, Claire is well-named. The insightful fool, the jester in their marital court, Claire has a need for safety far more embedded than that of the other characters; sitting on the sidelines rather than entering the field is the safest vantage point.

As the play provides yet another guided tour around the Albee arena of marriage, it examines the fairly retrograde gender roles of the American upper middle class: men make the money and the drinks and the decisions, and women make those decisions work. Agnes and Tobias have accommodated each other in highly civilized, ritualized ways. But, despite the clearly drawn and well-guarded parameters of that marital arena, there is intrusion—of Harry and Edna, of the Terror. (Julia's intrusion is a false disruption, a repetition of known circumstances, just as Claire's intrusion on their lives has assumed the level of permanence.) Albee's plays always turn on that moment of intrusion—the stranger in the park, the late-night party guests, the lizards from the sea—and the intruders tip the delicate balance. We learn the next morning, after Harry and Edna emerge, that the husbands, Harry and Tobias, have both come like intruders into their wives' beds; rather than renewing their intimacy, the intrusion confirms its loss, and the balance is, forlornly, once again restored.

Edna's sad but menacing question when they arrive, needing shelter from the existential Terror, is central to the outcome: "Friendship is something like a marriage, is it not, Tobias? For better or for worse?" (2:90). Although Tobias heroically tries to insist on his willingness to accept the "worse," the intimacy, however superficial, between the two couples will not be restored. When Agnes says to Edna, "Well, don't be strangers," Edna replies, "Oh, good Lord, how could we be? Our lives are . . . the same" (2:119). Forty years of friendship has revealed them to be strangers, and that is the dark weight of the play. Harry has rejected Tobias—both his offer of shelter and his love—and Agnes has rejected Edna's offer to resume their days in town together. Edna's astute insight, crucial to the meaning of the play, is surprising since it seems to be tossed off by a relatively minor character. She provides the key to the rejections: "It's sad to come to the end of it, isn't it, nearly the end [. . .] and still not know—still not have learned . . . the boundaries, what we may not do . . . not ask, for fear of looking in a mirror. We *shouldn't* have come" (2:118). The play would hold the mirror up to us, as well.

Box and *Quotations from Chairman Mao Tse-Tung*

Written as a conscious attempt "to expand the boundaries of the theatre," as Albee explains in his introduction to volume 2 of *The Collected Plays,* these two short plays can be presented separately but are intended to be combined into a three-part structure, with two-thirds of *Box* performed first, followed by all of *Quotations from Chairman Mao Tse-Tung,* with a short reprise of the final third of *Box* concluding the production. The entirety is referred to as *Box-Mao-Box.*

Box places us in a suburb of Beckettland; the audience looks at an empty box, and this evocative, albeit humorless, homage is filled only by the voice of a middle-aged woman. The cube should be designed, according to Albee's directions, to take up most of a small stage, with the cube's front side (i.e., fourth wall) removed so that we can see into it; its sides, top, and bottom should form slightly odd angles as they meet the back side. It is brightly lit. Thus the most obvious metaphoric value of the box is the stage: Albee has created a stage within a stage, although not a play within a play, since this is a stage without a play, a postapocalyptic theater that is nearly post-theater, where all that remains is a disembodied voice. The putative fourth wall, crucial to twentieth-century theatrical realism, is evoked when Voice refers to "six sides to bounce it all off of" (2:265).

The box is also reminiscent of images in other Albee plays: for example, Jerry's strongbox in *The Zoo Story*, which has no lock and contains "sea-rounded rocks"; the sandbox in *The Sandbox*, which is Grandma's coffin and which is, like the cube in *Box*, the image of the play's central meaning; and the boxes in *The American Dream* into which Grandma has packed her life, anticipating the arrival of "the van man," her Angel of Death. It is intriguing to contemplate the box's similarity to the model of the castle, another container within a container, in *Tiny Alice*.

Even more intriguing is Albee's experience of sculptural boxes: in his essay on Louise Nevelson (a longtime friend who became the sole character in his more recent play *Occupant*), he writes of his intense experience of sitting in the reconstruction of a room Mondrian had designed: "imagine a Mondrian painting twenty by twenty feet; then imagine it a cube; then imagine yourself placed in the center of the cube. . . . I had been transformed from spectator to participant" (*SMM*, 79–80). Nevelson's structure, *Mrs. N's Palace*, is a room, where one "literally enters Nevelson's world, is engulfed by it" (*SMM*, 79). It is crucial to note here that *Mrs. N's Palace* was inspired by *Tiny Alice*. This transformation "from spectator to participant" is, perhaps, what Albee means to do to us in *Box-Mao-Box*, placing Voice beside us rather than in front of us: "The voice should come not from the stage but should seem to be coming from nearby the spectator" (2:263).

Box's voice, described as "a Middle Western farm woman's voice," someone who is "fiftyish," begins somewhat implausibly right at the start by referring to a rocking chair as a *sedia d'ondalo* and then translates from the Italian for us. This introduces this unseen woman as pretentious; her formal rhetoric ("for that is Italian") contributes to that impression, as does her elitism as she confuses the artisan with the servant: "Oh, very good work; fine timber, and so fastidious, like when they shined the bottoms of shoes . . . *and the instep*" (2:264). This confusing characterization develops in curious and inconsistent ways; she continues, "The *Pope* warned us, he said so. There are no possessions, he said, so long as there are some with nothing we have no right to anything" (2:265). This putative person is an unlikely messenger, but, since her lament is the crux of the play, we must take her seriously. In mourning the loss of art and crafts, she greatly admires the handsome box—although the loss of carpentry and bread-making would seem ludicrously minor losses compared to the end of the world that she seems to be telling us about: "Seven hundred million babies dead in the time it takes, took, to knead the dough to make a proper loaf" (2:264).

She muses about "system as conclusion, in the sense of method as an end," an indictment of contemporary art as well as contemporary science, of process rather than product, the loss of meaning and moral purpose in the act of being able, merely, to invent. It is difficult to determine whether this is a warning or a dirge; is she suggesting that we, the audience, as representatives of civilization, can still save the world and all we value, or is she suggesting that the end has occurred and there is nothing to be done? Perhaps the strongest clue lies in her repeated reference to "spilling milk"; on the plot level, this would seem to refer to some heinous event in the recent past, if "past" still has meaning: "Or was it the milk? *That* may have been the moment: spilling and spilling and killing all those children to make a point. A penny or two, and a symbol at that, and I suppose the children were symbolic, too, though they died, and couldn't stop. Once it starts—gets to a certain point—the momentum is too much. But spilling milk! [. . .] Oh for every pound of milk they spill you can send a check to someone, but that does not unspill" (2:265) (*pound* of milk?). In the reprise, Voice tells us, "That is the thing about music. That is why we cannot listen anymore. *(Pause)* Because we cry" (2:298). Crying over spilled milk: the act of futility that suggests that there is, to quote Beckett's resonant first line of *Waiting for Godot*, "Nothing to be done." *Quotations from Chairman Mao Tse-Tung* goes on to support this conclusion.

One of the four characters, the Minister, is silent and dozing, presenting religious authority as blatantly inadequate, clearly asleep on the job. The other three characters—the Long-Winded Lady, the Old Woman, and Mao Tse-Tung—speak, but not to each other, not even hearing each other, which suggests their self-absorption and insularity. This continues to be true when Voice from *Box* joins them (aurally, but not, of course, in person). Our inclination is to try to make sense of the sequence of speeches, to make dialogue of the fragmented monologues, as both a theatrical and a human necessity, and see the ways these isolated voices echo each other. For example, the Old Woman's announcing the title of Will Carleton's sentimental nineteenth-century poem "Over the Hill to the Poor-House" is directly followed by Mao's dictum, "Poverty gives rise to the desire for change, the desire for action, the desire for revolution," which is rendered fatuous in context. When the Old Woman recites the poem's verse about moving into her daughter Susan's house, only "to discover that there wasn't room for me," the Long-Winded Lady tells us, "It's my daughter who will not see *me*, or rather, not often" (2:292). The Long-Winded Lady's long-winded monologue, interrupted by the other voices, has three main topics: her husband's dying and death (clearly a preview of Albee's next play, *All Over*), her own near-drowning by inexplicably falling overboard (attempted suicide? attempted murder?), and her walking out of a bakery, having bought hot crullers, just in time to see a taxi careen out of control and kill ten or twelve people.

Much of the intertextual resonance created by the two plays and by their isolated voices is oblique, but the ultimate effect is that these characters, oblivious of each other's presence, are linked by the play itself. Thus a paradox arises, demonstrating simultaneously their common humanity and their self-absorbed isolation, creating what Albee calls "the experiment: musical structure—form and counterpoint" (2:270). Albee's method of construction was, literally, cut and paste: "I put down the 'Over the Hill to the Poorhouse' poem in quatrains. Then I took the 'Quotations from Chairman Mao' in the order in which he wrote them. Then I took my scissors and I cut each quotation and kept them in exactly the same order. I did the Long-Winded Lady's monologue in paragraphs. I put all these things on walls around me, and I constructed the psychologically proper order for them to go in. [. . .] The order was governed by a sense of musical composition" (*ASJ*, 273–74).

This musical structure suggests the sonata form: theme and exposition, followed by development, followed by a recapitulation of the theme, although not necessarily identical to the original statement. In *Box*, Voice tells us, "Here is the thing about tension and the tonic—the important thing. *(Pause)* The release of tension is the return to consonance; no matter how far traveled, one comes back, not circular, not to the starting point, but a . . . setting down again, and the beauty of art is order—not what is familiar, necessarily, but order . . . on its own terms" (2:265). The return to the home key, to *Box*, would suggest that Voice is here describing the play that contains her.

Written in 1968, *Box-Mao-Box* premiered the following year. In 1970, Albee wrote an essay that recounts his recurring dream about the end of the world, which seems a likely source for the imagery of these postapocalyptic plays, although he himself does not suggest the link:

> It is a dream I have about once a year—a rather calm dream—and it cannot be fairly called a nightmare. For while the extinction of life on earth by fire and suffocation is nightmare material, the result of such a holocaust—the earth becoming like its moon—produces an intense sadness rather than terror.
>
> Nightmares are made of what has happened or what we can conceive happening. Dreams do not have to be.
>
> In this dream, I am on a beach by the ocean. It is dusk turning rapidly into night. I am with two or three friends, none of whom is anyone I can place on waking. We are lying about, and perhaps we have a driftwood fire smoldering. It is incredibly quiet—rather as if all sound had been turned off. And suddenly it begins: an area of the eastern horizon is lighted by the fired explosion, hundreds of miles away, and no sound at all. Then another, perhaps to the west, no sound. Within seconds they are everywhere, always at a great distance.
>
> To the three or four of us on the beach, before our smoldering fire, there is no question as to what is happening: we are watching the end of the world. There is no time for terror; it is overleaped, and the suddenness is unimaginable as the silent bombs go off. It will be seconds before our own lives cease—or maybe we are already dead; perhaps that is why there is no sound. (*SMM*, 61–62)

The "three or four of us" seem to have become *Box-Mao-Box*'s characters.

All Over

All Over is a compendium of Albee's favorite subjects: sex, death, and grammar among the country club set. Most of its characters, situations, and concerns seem to be either derived from or indicative of characters, situations, and concerns in other, better plays he wrote in the years preceding and subsequent to 1971. Yet there is enough drama and magisterial style here to hold our interest and to warrant a much-acclaimed revival in 2002, starring Rosemary Harris and directed by Emily Mann at McCarter Theatre. But, as Charles Isherwood noted in his admiring review of that production, the play "may leave many theatergoers with a feeling of having attended a requiem mass delivered in an arcane language."

The rhythm of the dialogue creates the play's arch and stylized realism, linguistically inventing the world these characters live in and that we share for the duration. Here is a good example as they discuss the dying man's opening and closing of his eyes, a characteristic gesture revealing his impatience:

> THE MISTRESS. It was always—for me—an indication that . . .
> THE DOCTOR *(No urgency)* Nurse.
> *(Some reaction from them all; not panic, but a turning of heads; a quickening)*

THE WIFE. Something?

THE DOCTOR. *(Looks up at them; a slight smile; some surprise)* Oh
. . . oh, *no.* Just . . . business.

(Slight pause)

THE MISTRESS. *(Not pressing, continuing)* an indication that . . . some
small fraction had gone out of him, some . . . faint shift from total
engagement. Or, if not that, a warning of it: impending. (2:311)

Characters who live at this level of subtlety of observation, noting and articulating such minute and precise distinctions, make
enormous demands on actors. Since there is so little action, their
voices, faces, and bodies need to convey nuances of meaning, reflecting how each feels about what he or she is saying and how, too, he or
she feels about the character addressed.

The man who is dying on the massive upstage bed—the famous
patriarch of this family—is the play's focus, but he is, in fact, never
seen. As the Wife says at the play's end, "All we've *done* is think
about ourselves. Ultimately" (2:366). And talk about themselves.
Only on rare occasions do these characters speak in actual dialogue;
their interactions are tellingly infrequent, and their self-absorption
tellingly insulating, so that much of the play's language is in the
form of miniature monologues that intersect, interrupt, or comment
on each other. The hothouse, ultracivilized atmosphere surrounding
the deathbed where they have gathered, according to ritual, to wait
for his end, is chilly; his dying is overseen by the ancient physician
("I am the most . . . general of practitioners") and tart-tongued nurse
(who turns out to have been an even more ancient physician's mistress) who provide punctuating reports of the patriarch's descent
toward death.

We meet the family: The wife of fifty years, the play's central
character, whom the patriarch long ago left—but did not divorce—for
the mistress; the relationship between the two women is by far the
most textured and interesting of the play. Minor but crucial voices
are the Best Friend, who is also the Wife's lover, the pallid Son who
works, none too happily, in the Best Friend's law firm, and the
obstreperous, needy Daughter (much like Julia in *A Delicate Bal-*

ance) who spitefully allows the press photographers and reporter to invade the room, causing the disruption that ends act 1. But even she, the least admirable and least sympathetic character, understands herself; as the Mistress wryly and accurately notes, "Nobody's a fool here" (2:338). There is rarely a fool to be found in an Albee play.

One of the Wife's most remarkable reminiscences is provoked by the Mistress, who says, "It's only the mother who can ever really know whose child it is." Laughing "gaily," the Wife replies that once her husband asked her, "*Did* I make these children? Was it *our* doing: the two of us alone?" Again laughing, she told him, "with some joy, for while we *were* winding down we were doing it with talk and presence: the silences and the goings off were later; the titans were still engaged: and I said, 'Oh, yes, my darling; yes, we did; they are our very own'" (2:314). This gives us a rich glimpse into their marriage, the Wife's sense of their rapport and style together—and thus the loss she has suffered in his leaving her. It provides, too, an ironic commentary on those very children, now both middle-aged and deeply disappointing to their mother. While she "chuckles quietly," the Daughter "rises, almost languidly," walks across the room, and slaps her mother across the face, "evenly, without evident emotion," following which the Wife "rises, just as languidly," walks over to the Daughter, and slaps her face, also "without evident emotion" (2:315). The play is sprinkled with these jaw-dropping emotional revelations, always through action rather than speech.

These violent punctuations of their urbane, elegant lives allow us to see below the smooth surface: the Son's sobbing against the wall when he returns from the bathroom, the Best Friend's account of his wife's growing madness ("Each thing, each . . . incident—uprooting all the roses, her hands so torn, so . . . killing the doves and finches . . . setting fire to her hair . . . all . . . all those times, those things I knew were pathetic, and not wanton, I watching myself withdraw, step back and close down some portion of," 2:312)—all provide a theatrically shocking contrast to the quiet inaction of the play. Most chilling is the women's response to the son's self-denigrating exposure: "And that is not what we meant at all," and, "No, not at all" (2:312). This nearly exact quotation from T. S. Eliot's "The Love Song of J. Alfred Prufrock" is cruel in its supercilious indictment of his inadequacy and his painful awareness of that inadequacy.

Perhaps most revelatory is the laughter shared by the Wife and the Mistress when, during the ongoing debate about whether to bury or cremate, the Best Friend, taking a quotation too literally, causes their "concert" of "cold, knowing, helpless laughter" (2:316). They laugh together again toward the close of act 1 when the Mistress tells the bizarre story of her grandfather. The Wife tries to say, "Poor man!" but is helpless with laughter. No sooner does she subside than she bursts out again; the Best Friend starts to giggle as well, and another burst of laughter starts everybody else laughing except the Daughter. The Wife and the Mistress have an arm around each other by the end. This "laughing wild amid severest woe" is true Beckettian laughter, what Albee describes in the stage directions as that "produced by extreme tension, fatigue, ultimate sadness and existentialist awareness" (2:331).

Sex and death are most blatantly united in the Doctor's chuckling reminiscence about his early days as a prison doctor: "There were some, in the final weeks, who had abandoned sex, masturbation, for God, or fear, or some enveloping withdrawal, but not all; some . . . some made love to themselves in a frenzy—indeed, I treated more than one who was bleeding from it, from so much—and several confided to me that their masturbation image was their executioner . . . some fancy of how he looked" (2:321). This grotesque image, delivered with such distantiation, continues as the Doctor remembers his longing for his grandson (or great-nephew), wishing to "lie in [his] long blond hair, put my lips there in the back of the neck," trying to explain to the Son "how we become enraptured by (Small smile) . . . the source of our closing down. You see I suddenly loved my executioners . . . well, figurative; and in the way of . . . nestling up against them, huddling close—for we do seek warmth, affection even, from those who tell us we are going to die, or when" (2:322). This betrayal is fundamental to Albee's sense of the human condition, where the life force, expressed sexually, wages war with death: the endless Freudian struggle between Eros and Thanatos.

At the play's conclusion, when it is literally "all over" for the unseen husband-lover-father-friend, we watch the Wife lose her aplomb, both revealing and, simultaneously, discovering her unhappiness. As her meltdown begins, her genteel, well-bred restraint breaks; it is "all over" for her, too: "*I* don't love *anyone. (Pause)* Any more" (2:365), except her husband, whom she has lost both to the Mistress and to death. She weeps at the final curtain because she is "unhappy." And once again, the Albee lesson, heard first in *The Zoo Story*, is reiterated: "What is gained is loss."

Albee's tone throughout creates the curious impression of admiration combined with contempt for this patrician world. When the Mistress muses, "Maybe that's how we keep the nineteenth century going for ourselves: pretend it exists" (2:324), we are struck by her acute self-knowledge, and the characters' melancholy revulsion at the "sad and shabby world we live in" (2:328). The Daughter, primary representative of that diminished modern world, accuses them of being "pious hypocrites"; she mistakes their elegant marital arrangements, their ornate and discreet infidelities for the crass sexual world she inhabits, a world of men who exploit her for her money and blacken her eyes; the resulting loss of self-respect has made her, in her mother's shrewd analysis, unlovable and unloving. Nonetheless, the Daughter's accusatory word "smug" hangs in the air. If "nobody's a fool here," nobody is very likable either, making *All Over* bitter and icily compelling.

Seascape

The cultural dispute about creationism versus evolution was everywhere in 2005, from university classrooms to TV's *Boston Legal* to movies about penguins. Much of the controversy focused on Dover, Pennsylvania, where a school board favoring the teaching of "intelligent design" (ID) was voted out (and where, astoundingly, Charles Darwin's great-great-grandson, journalist Matthew Chapman, was covering the federal trial), while in Kansas, teaching ID was mandated. A major new exhibit called "Darwin" opened at the American Museum of Natural History in New York the same weekend in November that *Seascape*'s Broadway revival opened.

The cartoons addressing ID would fill a hefty album; my favorite appeared in the *New Yorker*. It shows a fish in the sea, and, on the beach, a parade: first, an amphibian, then a dinosaur, then an ape, followed by a Neanderthal and ending finally in a man holding a book, which is probably a Bible. He looks over his shoulder at them and says, "Scram!" And another newcomer to the field, "Literary Darwinism," an academic fashion in literary criticism, maintains that literature can be read through biology and that fiction reveals our genetic predispositions, with Jane Austen's *Pride and Prejudice* functioning as the movement's template. Literary Darwinism is a subset of the field of biopoetics, which reads visual art and music through Darwinian theory.

In this charged atmosphere, *Seascape,* which won the 1975 Pulitzer Prize, the first of Albee's three Pulitzers, created even more interest than a major play by a major playwright with a major cast might be expected to receive, since *Seascape* is a play about evolution.

It begins with a married couple in late middle age finishing a picnic at the beach. Charlie and Nancy are unlike most of Albee's couples in their mildness and their kindliness to each other; the marital talk lacks the sharp edges we hear in many of the other plays. Charlie and Nancy are, however, typical of Albee's couples in several ways: they have been married many years, their children are grown, and they face the last portion of their lives with different desires: Charlie thinks they have "earned a little rest," while Nancy thinks they have "earned a little *life."* Her version of the wifely role is summed up in her unfinished sentence: "So, tell me what it is you want to do, and . . ." (2:374). The implied unspoken conclusion is, "I'll make it work," the line Agnes speaks to Tobias in *A Delicate Balance.* This capable female accommodation is the task of Albee wives, a role they always fulfill, although sometimes they chafe at the necessity. Thus, the initial debate between Charlie and Nancy is between action and stasis, the ease of what Nancy condemns as "the purgatory before the purgatory": "Well, why don't we act like the old folks [. . .] . Take our teeth out, throw away our corset, give in to the palsy, let our mind go dim, play lotto and canasta with the widows and the widowers, eat cereal [. . .] No thank you, sir!" (2:375).

Once again Albee examines the dangers of safety. The uneasy marital peace is disturbed by the arrival of Sarah and Leslie, two human-sized lizards who have emerged from the sea, impelled by some evolutionary imperative, a feeling they describe as "not belonging anymore." Their dis-ease, their feeling of "having changed," of no longer finding the watery realm "comfortable," inversely parallels Charlie's childhood longing to be a underwater creature. As a boy, he practiced holding his breath so he could sit on the bottom—first of a swimming pool, then of an ocean cove, then in the open sea—learning to stay under long enough for the "sand to settle and the fish [to] come back." The wished-for goal, he remembers, was ultimately achieved: "One stops being an intruder, finally—just one more object come to the bottom, or living thing, part of the undulation and the silence" (2:379). His boyhood experiments are an attempt to return to some prehuman state ("Gills, too?"), a temporary reversal of the evolutionary process, rejecting the human realm of air and noise. Charlie's longed-for cessation was to arrive at a condition of being of "just one more object come to the bottom [. . .] part of the undulation and the silence" (2:379). Nancy encourages his regressive wish, this devolutionary, backward longing, when she urges her husband to recapture his sensual pleasure and "be young again."

It is no accident that in the one bad time in their marriage, years before, when Charlie fell into a "seven-month decline," spending all his time "rereading Proust," Nancy flirted with a solution: "I can have me a divorce, I thought, become eighteen again" (2:383). This is a very Proustian wish, the desire to recapture lost time. Charlie reveals that his sexual fantasies centered not on another person but on another occasion: "I pretended it was the time before, and it was quite good that way" (2:384).

Central to Charlie's fishlike yearnings is that "one stops being an intruder, finally." The "intruder" is thematic in Albee, and *Seascape* is paradigmatic. In both the earlier works, *A Zoo Story* and *A Delicate Balance*, and the later work, *The Play About the Baby*, the intruders bring an end of innocence, wrecking the inhabitants' contented, self-deluding security. In *Seascape*, the intruders are Sarah and Leslie, who have already felt themselves to be intruders in their own realm, their former underwater home. Having emerged onto land, they become intruders into the human realm. The sea creatures, having discovered consciousness and having learned about mortality, cannot retreat to a bicameral mind-state; the arrow of time with its inevitable trajectory is the undeniable fact of life on earth.

In an interview with Stephen Bottoms, Albee warned against making the lizards "cute" ("Borrowed Time," 245). In any major production of this play, the costume designer who creates the lizard suits is the secret star of the show, needing to make costumes that will astonish us without making us laugh or cringe, lest the show's "reality . . . fade away." For the Broadway revival, Catherine Zuber created two gorgeous skins for Elizabeth Marvel and Frederick Weller. Somewhere between iguana and Gila monster, they were both beautiful and shockingly reptilian, nearly jeweled in their green brilliance. The two actors developed saurian moves, slithering downhill, elbows akimbo, heads turning in sharp, alert jerks. The moment when we see them appear at the crest of the dune, before Charlie and Nancy notice them (they are too involved in their squabbling—and what a marital lesson lies there) is eye-widening, even if we know the play and know in advance the lizards' entrance is about to happen.

"Progress is a set of assumptions," Charlie tells Leslie. Despite the apparent rejoicing at progress—the cosmic advancement from "primordial soup" to "that heartbreaking second when it all got together, the sugars and the acids and the ultraviolets, and the next thing you knew there were tangerines and string quartets" (2:439)— a warning is sounded by the play's first sound effect: jet planes overhead, intruders in the natural beauty and calm. The play's first spoken line is, "Such noise they make," and Charlie replies to Nancy, "I don't know what good they do," ushering in the evolution/devolution debate that is the heart of the play. Just as this antimodern, antitechnology note is sounded, Nancy exclaims, "Can't we stay here forever?" This sounds more antievolutionary than Nancy is; by "here" she means the world's beaches, fantasizing about following an endless summer and becoming "seaside nomads," suggesting adventure rather than static primitivism. Nancy says to Charlie, "You have to be pushed into everything" (2:373), an observation both personal and Darwinian. Nancy has none of Charlie's reactionary nostalgia for some prehuman state; her instinctive desire has always been to go forward rather than back, to be eager rather than reluctant: "When *I* was little [. . .] I wanted to be *woman*" (2:377).

Gender roles are crucial to this play; females of any species are, according to *Seascape,* far more tolerant, curious, and imaginative— with occasional lapses into ingenuous cuteness and petulance. The male of any species is, according to Albee, competitive, self-important, and dependent on the female in any negotiation with danger.

Gender roles are comically (and clichédly) presented in Leslie's sexual bragging, his pride in his tail, his protectiveness of Sarah. But despite these gender roles, the crux of the play lies in Albee's attempt to define the essence of the human: using tools, making art, achieving consciousness of mortality. Leslie stumbles, on his own, into the Cartesian assumption: "I *think* I exist," although the play is, finally, disappointing in its lack of philosophic depth.

Depth is, after all, the metaphor of the play; the lizards' emergence from the depths of the sea suggests but does not satisfyingly deliver meaning. One tempting interpretation is that the action of the play is about the development of civilization: but since Leslie and Sarah are eminently civilized linguistically, ethically, and behaviorally, the idea that they are undeveloped and unsocialized seems a false one. Or, one could argue that we are watching characters arranged along a chronological spectrum of human development, that Leslie and Sarah are Charlie and Nancy before the fact of their being fully human. Albee would seem, then, to have created characters who are both themselves and everyone, both particular personalities as well as representatives of the human condition, as he so often does, underscoring his characters' universality by giving them only generic names. His timeline characters in *Three Tall Women* suggest this evolution of personality, where one becomes oneself over time: A is the old woman, the ur-personality, while B is the middle-aged women she was earlier in her life, and C is the young woman from whom she develops. Their life is filled with specific stories and attitudes and events, but they also represent the inevitable process of aging, of remembering and forgetting, of self-invention that is a larger, more generalized portrait of the human. Another way of viewing this chronological spectrum is mythically, to see the lizards in a prelapsarian state, before modesty was invented, where the female creature is the curious one.

Another possible reading is that the lizards emerge from below the level of consciousness, from the depths of the unconscious mind. But Leslie and Sarah have traveled from their own earlier, primal states to the condition that impelled them to the surface and then to the liminal condition in which we meet them; they have been following a continuum from the instinctual to the fully socialized. As Nancy tells the lizards, who are ready to retreat from the world, "You'll have to come back . . . sooner or later. You don't have any choice. Don't you know that? You'll have to come back up" (2:447). It is worth noting that the stage directions support this idea, indicating rising motion; since the dune is specified as having a "ridge" and a "pinnacle" (a word, laden with significance, which we will hear again in *The Goat*), they ascend as the play concludes. Most significant is the unexpected happy ending as the lizards accept the biological imperative and the human help offered by Nancy and Charlie. Just how optimistic *Seascape*'s conclusion is can be measured by how far Albee departs from the Beckettian vision: when Leslie asks with "anger and doubt" how Charlie and Nancy could help, Charlie ("sad, shy") replies, "*Take* you by the hand?" (2:448). This literalizing of the helping hand echoes, but distinguishes itself from, Beckett's *All That Fall*, when Maddy Rooney asks "the dark Miss Fitt" for aid climbing stairs, only to be met with incomprehension: "Is it my arm you want Mrs. Rooney or what is it?" and Mrs. Rooney fumes in despair: "Your arm! Any arm! A helping hand! For five seconds! Christ, what a planet!" This gesture of reaching out has earlier been used for comic ends in *Seascape:* Nancy decides they should greet the lizards "properly" by shaking hands, leading to a delightful commotion over designations of arm and leg, fingers and toes.

The helping hand extended at the end of *Seascape* seems to ameliorate Albee's vision, although he himself insists that the play's final exchange, ending with the word "Begin," is far less benevolent: "It's a threat. It's really a threat. [. . .] Leslie turns around and says, 'OK, buddy, begin.' Meaning, 'and if you don't succeed, I'll rip you to pieces.' That's the whole intention of that last line. If you misunderstand that, then it's a misunderstanding of the play as profound as many misunderstandings of *Our Town*" ("Borrowed Time," 245).

As frequently happens in an Albee play, the events turn on the uses of language by characters whose linguistic sense is acute. When Charlie tells Nancy, "You've had a good life," she becomes hurt and irritated by his use of the past tense:

NANCY. Yes! Have *had*! What *about* that!

CHARLIE. What about it!

NANCY. *Am* not *having. (Waits for reaction; gets none)* Am not *having*? Am not *having* a good life?

CHARLIE. Well, of *course*!

NANCY. Then why say had? Why put it that way?

CHARLIE. It's a way of speaking!

NANCY. No! It's a way of thinking! *I* know that language, and I know *you*. You're not careless with it, or didn't used to be. (2:389)

The complexity of linguistic designations is intensified when nouns move to the abstract. Trying to explain human attitudes toward children, Nancy tells Sarah, "We *love* them," only to be asked to explain what the word means. When she tells the lizards that love is "one of the emotions," they are puzzled by this new word, responding as true Albee characters, "We'll never know unless you define your terms. Honestly, the imprecision!" (2:419). Ultimately the explanation is theatrical rather than academic, it is *shown*: Charlie makes Sarah cry at the thought of never seeing Leslie again, and thus she learns what the word means by internalizing its definition; words mean viscerally as well as intellectually, and allowing us to imagine what has not happened is one of the great functions of language in human life. It is also one of the functions of theater.

Although half the cast are giant lizards, *Seascape* has none of the Kafkaesque elements one would expect, neither Kafka's grim and terrifying vision nor his guilt-laden, inscrutable atmosphere. It does, however, participate in the deadpan grotesque that is the hallmark of "The Metamorphosis," also about a huge, shocking, allegorical, anthropomorphized creature. In fact, Albee refers to the play as one of his "straightforward [plays]—naturalistic, one might say, except that there is no such thing as naturalism in the theatre, merely degrees of stylization" (2:8). In Kafka, the naturalistic in the face of the overwhelmingly outlandish creates the trademark stylization that simultaneously refuses stylization. Comparison of *Seascape* with "A Report to an Academy," Kafka's story about a talking ape, may be apt, since that story satirically suggests precisely what Albee's thumbnail interpretation of the play suggests: "*Seascape* wonders whether we are an evolving species or perhaps a devolving one" (2:9). As in Kafka's story, individual development encapsulates and demonstrates Darwinian evolution; in both works, the authors wonder whether progress—with its implications of positive forward motion—is merely a self-consolatory myth. Further, the play and the story share a sense of melancholy, as the character's irremediable exile from his former state evokes a nostalgia for an irretrievable past. It is the lizards who are the Proustian characters.

Seascape makes a plea for tolerance that is fundamental to Albee's vision. Leslie says, "Being different is interesting; there's nothing implicitly inferior or superior about it. *Great* difference, of course, produces natural caution; and if the differences are too extreme . . . well, then, reality tends to fade away" (2:426). The resonance here seems, at first glance, to be social commentary about Otherness—gender, sexual preference, race—especially since Leslie has just revealed his bigotry about fishes. But Leslie's insight may be a comment on the play itself. The risk in making half your cast giant lizards is that "reality tends to fade away," but the play shows us that even giant lizards are "interesting" and that even our "natural caution" like Charlie's and Nancy's, vanishes with openness, tolerance, willingness, kindness. As Albee told Bigsby, "*Seascape* is a completely realistic play. Absolutely naturalistic. It is merely a speeded-up examination of the processes of evolution. . . . It is not a theoretical play. . . . It is very much an act of aggression, and very public" (316–17). This last remark suggests that, no matter how hidden, Albee's political agenda is always there, making all theater an act of aggression against an audience's inclination to conformity and passivity.

Listening

Listening is about listening; the Girl complains that no one listens to her—and she is, sometimes, right—and in so doing echoes what may be everyone's secret complaint: we beg for attention, for love, for help, and nobody listens. It is difficult, though, to identify with a whiner, and the Girl, no matter how much she claims our attention and sympathy, is annoying. Like so many of Albee's plays, *Listening* both offers and withholds sympathy for its characters; each of *Listening*'s three characters is both likable and not, interesting and tedious, victim and victimizer. It is this complexity of tone, Albee's refusal to sentimentalize or to condemn, that makes for real realism, despite the artificiality of the play's structure and mode of presentation. And, of course, by extension, the title exhorts us to listen.

Listening is so cleverly constructed that it can be performed either as a stage play or as a radio play. It was commissioned for the radio, and Albee played Voice in its premiere production in 1976—as he was to do many years later in the New York revival of *Counting the Ways*; if the audience recognized his voice, it carried a special authority over the characters, literalizing the playwright's making them talk. The Voice's function in *Listening* is to number the scenes, a tantalizing notion of chronological order in a play that resists chronological order. As the Woman tells the Man, "The nonsequential is probably the most difficult to adjust to" (2:516). We, as readers, auditors, or spectators, are asked to remember clues, accept the apparent illogic of the psychological, to "retain," as the Woman demands of the Man when he forgets the significance of "sky blue" as the color of the Girl's cardboard. "Can't you retain?" she asks. He replies, "Well, mostly; not . . . *some* things; the perverse, the obscure, the out of kilter" (2:482). Albee requires precisely that, that we retain the perverse, the obscure, and the out of kilter—the content of this play—in order to understand *Listening*.

The play begins with the Man setting the scene by describing what he sees, matching it up against what was "promised," or "stated," or "announced," or "imagined," or "suggested." So whether we are listening to his description of the fountain or looking at it as part of the set design, we know where he is. We hear about the sounds as he imagines they would have been heard in the past: a footfall, "what a sound, echoing out of doors like that," and he muses about the "silence of the grass after all that echoing." These opening lines conclude with, "All right, *I'm* here. Where are *you?* Where *are* you? Be here, she said: *I'll* show you something! *(Chuckles. Pause. More sober)* [. . .] Ah! Finally! *(Calls)* Hel-loo!" (2:454). What is happening is clear in either medium, as it is, of course, to the reader.

The next scene begins, by contrast, with visuals: "Be here, you said. *I'll* show you something," followed by the Man's compliment to the Woman, "You're *look*ing well" (2:454). Thus the play's duality is embedded in its architecture as well as its meaning. This duality of the visual and auditory becomes even more significant by the play's end, when it is what the Woman and the Man have failed to see—represented by the shard of glass or whatever it is with which the Girl cuts herself. The choreographed focus of this scene distracts us from the Girl by directing our attention to the Man and Woman's conversation. She narrates, radio fashion, a event that may have taken place, "many years ago," when a girl, having approached her while reading in the park (note the similarity to *The Zoo Story*) asked, "Do you want me to *show* you something?" She then takes her hands out of her "deep fur pockets" to reveal that she has slashed her wrists. The Woman, the stage directions tell us, "demonstrates, very slowly" while the Man is riveted, as we are, by this narrated drama. "See?" the Woman says the girl said (2:515–16). But of course, we do not see, we *hear* this past event.

Albee's stage directions immediately following this are crucial: "Pause. The GIRL, who has been preparing the event behind the lip of the fountain, offers her hands over the edge, in the manner of the girl described above. Her hands are covered with blood" (2:516). The Girl then says to them (and, of course, to us), "Like this?" And, when they do not notice—although certainly the audience's attention has already radically shifted to her—she adds, "Please? Like this?" (2:517). This is a play about looking and listening—the fundamental demands any serious playwright makes on the audience, as well as the fundamental demands any serious person makes on us—and thus this radio/stage play is about making drama as well as about human relationships.

On one level, we are invited to construct a coherent narrative by rummaging around in the ambiguities and allusions to the past the characters offer. We may, for example, assume that the Girl is the child of a long-ago liaison between the Man and the Woman—who— perhaps—once held hands, sometime after she made him cry. Perhaps the Man is the cook at the institution where the Girl is kept ("I do your food"), or the Woman is her therapist. The Girl seems to need to be restrained, having struck another inmate who looked, perhaps covetously, at her blue cardboard. This other inmate is, perhaps, "the September girl" who is incarcerated because she murdered her baby in some cast-off reality, having said, "Reality is too small for me." The Girl may have been committed to the institution because she tried to kill herself by slashing her wrists—an act repeated at the end of the play that may cause her death shortly after the curtain falls—or this dramatic climax may be simply a theatrical reenactment that, of course, occurs every night of the run of a production.

In any event, the Woman's remark to the Man, "It's an old vaudeville act now . . . except not very funny, and . . . thin of reason. Familiar? Familiar territory?" (2:485), seems nearly a description of the play that is often jokey without being humorous ("Well, you never *know*. You know?"). Our attempts to excavate the backstory are futile, however, and we are left with the play that may be more experimental construct than drama. We can extract ideas from the text, although the unsettling ambiguities seem more contrivance than dramatic necessity.

Listening's subtitle is *A Chamber Play,* which implies that it is better suited to an intimate performing space than to a large theater, but as a radio play, this "chamber" may be the listener's home, calling to mind old-fashioned images of people sitting around the radio in their living room, their eyes focused on the middle distance, imagining what they hear. The subtitle also suggests the play's affinity with chamber music, aspiring to create its emotional effects by the interplay of the voices or instruments—perhaps a string trio. It may be that the atmospheric but inconclusive *Listening* is best heard in this way.

Counting the Ways: A Vaudeville

How do I love thee? Let me count the ways.
I love thee to the depth and breadth and height
My soul can reach, when feeling out of sight
For the ends of Being and ideal Grace.
I love to the level of everyday's
Most quiet need, by sun and candlelight.
I love thee freely, as men strive for Right,
I love thee purely, as they turn from Praise.
I love thee with the passion put to use
In my old griefs, and with my childhood's faith.
I love thee with a love I seemed to lose
With my lost saints—I love thee with the breath,
Smiles, tears, of all my life!—and, if God choose,
I shall but love thee better after death.

Sonnet XLIII by Elizabeth Barrett Browning is one of the most famous love poems in the language, and every one of the ways she counts is recounted by Albee in this funny, moving play, both melancholic and cheerful, both parodic and earnest. The distance between Barrett Browning's Victorian sensibility and Albee's late-twentieth-century American sensibility is both the point and the pain. What is gained, once again, is loss, and the debits and credits are tallied, as various ways of loving and enduring are re-counted as well as recounted.

The play, like the poem, begins with a question: She asks He, "Do you *love* me?" She repeats the question with, according to the stage directions, even more emphasis on the word "love." It is both interesting and amusing to consider the changes that occur when emphasis is placed on each of the words: *Do* you love me? or Do *you* love me? or Do you *love* me? or Do you love *me*? This temptation to count the ways permeates the dialogue. The man's response is suspicious: "Why do you ask?" Her considered reply is, "Well: because I want to know." His reply is a question: "Right now?" which sets up an implied ambiguity (i.e., is the issue the loving or the knowing "right now"?). This seems ultimately resolved when he answers—after many comic pauses—with, "Of course." The play's final scene creates the perfect bookend to this introduction with a matching interrogation: He asks She as "a half-amused afterthought," "Do you love me?" and She replies, "I don't *know* . . . I *think* I do" (2:554).

This much-repeated question is the heart of the play: how do we bear the asking or the answering, burdened as He and She are by romantic notions of love (viz. Elizabeth Barrett Browning)? The repetitions are fundamental to the play—and to marriage, of course, creating a motif of habit. Thus the play's many scenes are like snapshots, and we leaf through the talking photo album of this couple's civilized life. When She asks He near the end of the play (in a manner described by Albee's stage directions as "bitter and hopeful simultaneously"), "Do you cheat on me a lot?" he replies, after the significant pause, "No; I don't. Good phrasing" (2:553), satisfying both her bitterness and her hopefulness simultaneously. The wordplay between these two highly verbal people is mainly about food and sex, both literal and metaphoric, and language is, as it always is in Albee's plays, a weapon—both for assault and for self-defense.

The passage of time is counted and measured in years married, in children (three or four?), in failing memory, in moments of abstraction, in loss of focus. The roses ("They're going to wilt! They're going to wilt!") become emblematic of the condition—both mortal and marital. The grammatical equivalent of this condition—of the human need to tote up time—is the verb mood called the historical present, which by narrating the past as if it were the present seems to erase time. She notes that it is "an odd tense, isn't it—sort of common, if you know what I mean. It's useful, I know, but . . . *still*" (2:541). He uses the historical present when he expresses his dismayed amazement over their separate beds: "All of a sudden there are two beds. Once upon a time there was one. [. . .] I wake up this morning in our king-size bed, the one I've waked in every day for all our marriage. [. . .] When did it happen? When did our lovely bed . . . split and become two?" (2:541–42). She replies, "Well, I suspect it's been coming. [. . .] it happens sooner or later; look around you; look at our friends. Sooner or later it happens. Maybe we'll be lucky and it won't go any further. [. . .] Separate rooms" (2:543).

If the historical present reverses time in one direction, "premature grief" reverses it in the other. Her longest speech, one that only seems to be too superficial to warrant so much space and time in so short a play, is about seating protocol at a dinner party her sister is giving. The dilemma involves the seating of two men who are terminally ill. Although She takes us through all the options of decorously honoring the men who are dying by seating them at the hostess's right hand, the problem remains that the hostess has only one right hand. All the "old questions about veneer" allow us realize that the superficiality of this weighty speech is only apparent. It is preceded by a clever and pointed introduction: at the beginning of scene 15, He is about to launch into a discussion of "premature grief" when She interrupts him with "Not yet! Not yet!," an attempt to forestall the emotional issue with the protocol issue; they are, of course, the same issue, since the seating dilemma hinges on "premature grief" (2:545).

Much earlier in the play, She, "bitter and resentful" about their sex life, describes her repugnance with his sexual aging, and suddenly adds, "And think about hence!! There are two things: cease and corruption. And that's all there is to say about hence!" (2:525). The play will examine deterioration—both physical and conjugal—and if there is nothing more to say about "hence," there is much to say about whence. "Here's a thought; I think it was my grandmother's; *love* doesn't die; we pass *through* it" (2:527). That wise grandmother, whom we have met before in *The Sandbox* and *The American Dream*, is an emissary from the past. After a comical conversation about what "love in the afternoon" means, She adds, "Love in the afternoon may be one thing, and love in the morning very much the same; they may both be dirty games, but love at night . . . oh, that has to be love." She concludes this conversation with, "What time is it?" (2:528).

Counting the Ways's subtitle is significant; *A Vaudeville* describes not merely the play's theatrical style, but its attitude, its tone, its vision, one central to the many marriage plays Albee had, by 1977, already written and those he would still write. With only two characters and a bare minimum of a set, *Counting the Ways* had its unfortunate premiere in London at the cavernous Olivier Theatre in the National, where it took seventy minutes instead of the forty minutes it should take. It was after this dreary and protracted first production that Albee added the subtitle as a clue to the play's nature, hoping to free it from the dangers of what Albee called "leaden sentimentality" (*ASJ*, 296).

In an essay called "About Theatre Language," published with the script of *The Last Yankee* in 1994, Arthur Miller makes a startling observation about the nature of vaudeville. Discussing Samuel Beckett's *Waiting for Godot,* he tells us that "the dominating theme of *Godot* is stasis and the struggle to overcome humanity's endless repetitious paralysis before the need to act and change." He cites the famous exchange when Pozzo finds himself unable to exit, despite many adieus, and, after a silence says, "I don't seem to be able . . . *(long hesitation)* . . . to depart." Estragon replies, "Such is life." Miller's commentary could serve as a gloss on Albee as well: "This is vaudeville at the edge of the cliff, but vaudeville anyway, so I may be forgiven for being reminded of Jimmy Durante's ditty—'Didja ever get the feelin' that you wanted to go? But still you had the feelin' that you wanted to stay?'" (90–91).

The Beckett connection is significant here, since the 2003 revival of *Counting the Ways* in New York was as the fourth piece in a program that began with three short plays by Beckett (*Not I, A Piece of Monologue,* and *Footfalls*). Albee is fond of pointing out that his career began with a similar pairing: *The Zoo Story* premiered in Berlin in a double bill with *Krapp's Last Tape*. When asked about Beckett's influence on his work Albee replied, "We learn from our betters," and in an address to the Beckett Society in Philadelphia in December 2004, Albee marveled at a Beckett line, "out there in the dark vast," noting that "a lesser playwright would have said 'vast dark.'"

Consider *Counting the Ways*'s subtitle, too, in light of Albee's grandfather, E. F. Albee, the vaudeville king of the 1920s who owned many vaudeville houses and made the family's fortune in show business. His vaudeville slogan was, "Always something for everybody." If we apply this motto to the present case, *Counting the Ways* becomes vaudevillian in ways larger than style. Its style is, of course, the play's most startling and entertaining feature. Albee creates deliberate tension between the realistic domestic conversation and the deliberate dismantling of the fourth wall of theatrical realism: at the start, a sign reading "COUNTING THE WAYS" drops to an empty stage, and then, after a few seconds, rises. After the blackout, scene 1 begins. At the play's conclusion, the narrative voice-over announces "THE END." From time to time, the characters feel self-conscious when they notice the audience; for example, He explains to She why he ate the remains of the rose—he had been "counting" the petals for she-loves-me-she-loves-me-not—"when, all at once I saw I was being watched . . . out *there*!" (2:530). Perhaps the funniest example of this self-reflexivity comes at the end of the entre-scene between scenes 14 and 15 when the offstage voice asks the actors to identify themselves. After each stands and talks with the audience, He asks She, "Where are you going?" and she replies, "Off" (2:545), leaving him sitting alone onstage.

The script's insistence that each actor provide an extemporaneous autobiographical chat, an "improvisation," is disingenuous in a performance repeated eight times each week. Although much of the play depends on the violation of the "fourth wall," the deliberate flouting of the barrier between stage and audience, Albee's erasure of that other, more complex wall between actor and character is far more intricate. In the 2003 New York production, the voice-over that sternly required the actors playing He and She to speak to us as them-selves was Albee's own recorded voice, thus underscoring—perhaps too drolly—the ultimate authority of the playwright, who controls, even when pretending not to control, what his actors say. Albee has never tolerated actors who take liberties with the text. As he said during the "Playwrights Panel" at the Last Frontier Theatre Confer-ence in Valdez, Alaska, in 2002: "There is one solution to the prob-lem of working with actors: write a mime play." Although he fre-quently quips about the struggle between actors and playwright for power over the script, his jokes betray a deep wariness of entrusting his work to others, an unavoidable necessity in an inherently collab-orative medium. This witticism also reveals his idea of a play: its existence is in its words, not in physical action.

When He muses, after playing with and diminishing a line from an Auden poem, "But if parody *isn't* a diminishment . . . well, then, was it worth it in the first place?" (2:538). The antecedent of "it" is a rich problem. *Counting the Ways* is filled with parody, especially self-parody as both a defense and an acknowledgment, a taking one-self seriously and, simultaneously, not, just as it is in the long, sad story of why there is no crème brûlée. Like the intuitive leap from his request for "Idiot's Delight" to her understanding that what he means is "Raspberry Fool," the play is filled with coded equivalents (love in the afternoon = sex, "lips" = "hips"). The linguistic equiva-lent of parody is the pun, which is, in Albee's language, usually gram-matically based. For example, when She swats him with the roses, saying, "These will wilt," He muses, "Wilt they will" (2:537). Puns, like parody, depend on the brain "panicking, sending out contradic-tory impulses" (2:538) so that when the stage directions read, "Pre-occupied; at a loss" (2:538), the word "loss" reverberates for readers as our brains panic. Another poetic parody, more oblique than the Auden, is She's nostalgic recounting of her going to a prom as a teenager. Holding the roses, she remembers the nauseating scent of the gardenias, and the humiliated boy who brought her a second cor-sage. "Some of us—believe it; try to believe it—some of us at seven-teen were, oh shame, I suppose to present eyes, still maidens, still maidens, head and hood" (2:534). The A. E. Housman overtones here tempting:

WITH rue my heart is laden
For golden friends I had,
For many a rose-lipt maiden
And many a lightfoot lad.

By brooks too broad for leaping
The lightfoot boys are laid;
The rose-lipt girls are sleeping
In fields where roses fade.

She interrupts her prom story with a glance down at the flowers in her hand: "These roses will wilt. Ah, well" (2:535).

He contemplates going mad: "There's something thrilling to the mind going. As with deafness—all the encroachments. Or can less encroach?" (2:533). Less has been encroaching since Albee put pen to paper. And like Agnes in *A Delicate Balance* contemplating her own loss of mind, there is a parodic attitude toward one's diminution. There is also gestural parody; perhaps the most resonant example occurs when He "looks at his rose, holds it at stiff arm's length toward her exit, closes his eyes tight" and says, "Here" (2:534). This is further parodied in the next scene, tiny scene 11, in which He "makes a grimace, extends, shakes his flower-held arm even further" and says "HERE!" The stage directions that follow are "Nothing happens."

This presentation of flowers visually parodies Chagall's many rose-filled, lover-filled paintings, and the gap between the two images is filled by longing as well as by cynicism. The rose gesture is, simultaneously, a genuinely romantic offering and a parody of it: a parody is not an inversion, but a falling off of meaning, which is, literarily, also an adding on of meaning. He's gestures also echo the gesture of the boy at the prom in She's memory, a recollection that is both bitter and sweet. He's gesture also recalls George offering his bouquet of snapdragons to Martha in *Who's Afraid of Virginia Woolf?* That, too is a partial parody of a genuine romantic love offering (see the discussion of *Who's Afraid of Virginia Woolf?*). All these parodies are diminutions of the original, but also testimony to how each is, as He puts it, "worth it in the first place"; each borrows, with a bittersweet yearning, the emotion that made the predecessor great. There is, of course, throughout, the longing for gesture—a staple of the theatrical art—to truly, deeply *mean*. This, finally, reveals Albee's awareness of the loss of straightforward, realistic, genuine, undeconstructed, unself-conscious gesture in contemporary theater.

The Lady from Dubuque

Of all the Albee characters who are difficult to warm up to, those who populate *The Lady from Dubuque*, are the most difficult—in fact impossible. Albee worked on the play for many years, and, when the script was finally ready, one famous actress after another (Ingrid Bergman and Colleen Dewhurst, among others) refused the role of Elizabeth. When it finally opened in New York, starring Irene Worth, it was savaged by the critics and closed after twelve performances.

It is no wonder that this play is rarely performed, although 2007 saw two revivals, one at Seattle Repertory Theatre, and one in London's West End with Dame Maggie Smith in the title role. The reviews from London (March 21, 2007) were mixed. All were admiring of Smith, but some were hardly less scathing than the reviews of the original production. The London critics called it "a clapped out, second rate play" (Charles Spencer in the *Telegraph*) and "sub-Pirandello and recycled Albee" (Paul Tayler in *The Independent*). "Despite the best efforts of Anthony Page's fine cast," wrote Benedict Nightingale in *The Times*, "I remained pretty much unimplicated and, worse, uninvolved throughout." "The play's real difficulty lies with the strain—in every sense—of artificiality in the writing," said David Richards in *Variety*. On the positive side, Michael Billington *(The Guardian)* wrote, "Seeing it now in London in Anthony

Page's silk-smooth production, I was simultaneously tantalised, intrigued, and entertained," while Matt Wolf, reviewing for Bloomburg.com wrote, "Even without the two-time Oscar winner in Albee's title role, the piece would still be essential viewing." And thus Albee's ability to roil the theatrical establishment continues unabated.

The group of friends we meet in the first scene playing parlor games—both actual and figurative—are people so heavily defended by sarcasm that, despite their troubles, sympathy from audiences and readers is in short supply. The play reeks of contempt for its characters and, it would seem, for humankind generally. In his introduction to volume 2 of *The Collected Plays*, Albee writes, "*The Lady from Dubuque* deals with the question of whether our reality is determined by our need and is not an absolute" (2:8). This is a pertinent reminder that theater, by its very illusion-creating nature, is a challenge to reality, although the fourth-wall bashing here in the play's arch asides to the audience try to force us into a complicity we may not accept. Addressing the audience is a technique Albee experiments with frequently, from the early *Sandbox*, to *Box* and *Quotations from Chairman Mao Tse-Tung*, to *The Play About the Baby*, and to *The Occupant*, where the entire play is a monologue addressed to the audience.

Lady harks back to the "fun and games" of *Who's Afraid of Virginia Woolf?*, where the game-playing is far more interesting and reveals far more about characters for whom, despite their flaws, we feel immense sympathy. George's and Martha's need for a child has invented a child, while in *Lady* Jo's need seems to have conjured up a mother to help her through the last stages of the cancer from which she is dying.

In the same way, *The Lady from Dubuque* looks forward to the more recent *The Play About the Baby*, where the young and innocent couple's need to deny tragic loss—both of their baby and of their innocence—conjures up the couple who serve as agents of experience, who seem to both cause and lessen their pain.

Both *The Play About the Baby* and *The Lady from Dubuque* turn on the appearance of a mysterious and powerful middle-aged couple who may or may not exist on the same level of reality as the younger people, just as both plays turn on the theme of betrayal, frequently explored in Albee plays. In *Lady*, the betrayal seems at first to be the obvious kind: friend's cruelty to friend (literalized near the play's end in their beating Sam and refusal to untie him), lover's cruelty to partner, and general jokiness of the malicious, adolescent variety. Jo, in her early thirties, is dying of what seems to be cancer—a betrayal both by her body and of her body. Sam, her devoted husband, has become possessive of her caretaking, and we will eventually see the self-righteousness that accompanies such terrible and exhausting attendance. He helplessly betrays her by trying to keep her from dying, thus prolonging her suffering.

When the imperious Elizabeth, the Lady from Dubuque, arrives, accompanied by her companion, Oscar, who seems to be a variation on the Angel of Death from the early *Sandbox*, they refuse to explain to Sam who they are; this central scene is so protracted and so arch that it sounds like an unfunny lampoon of an Albee play. Explaining Elizabeth and Oscar as surreal—or symbolic, or hallucinatory—figures does not mean they successfully function dramatically. The point of Oscar's being African-American—his race is the subject of much of the play's self-consciously haughty humor—is unclear. That he is physically formidable may be a satiric commentary on racial stereotyping, or simply racial stereotyping.

Albee told his biographer that the play shows that "our identity is created by other people's need for our identity to exist. Our existence depends on our usefulness" (*ASJ*, 310). These notions of "need" and "usefulness" would seem to justify the "existence" of Elizabeth and Oscar. If the reader-spectator identifies with any of the play's characters, it is likely to be Sam, the person who is helpless in the face of great suffering, despite his desire to be "useful." The real problem Albee has set for himself is how to write a play about characters who, as Jo describes them, are "unworthy of human solicitude" (2:646).

Lady and *Baby* share tonal as well as thematic similarities, the most dominant of which is Albee's philosophizing, so simplistic that it suggests his disdain extends to his audience. Elizabeth says, "Good, then we are not talking about the rights we pretend to give ourselves in this bewildered land of ours—life, liberty, and the pursuit of the unattainable—through we *may* be learning our limits—finally—here in the . . . last of the democracies" (2:657).

Albee has updated some of the topical references through the years:

> One character accuses another of being a "reactionary, Nixon-loving fag-hater." When *The Lady from Dubuque* was first staged, Jimmy Carter was in his final year in the White House and Nixon, though exiled in disgrace for six years, remained code for Republican extremism. For subsequent productions, Albee realigned his dialogue with the White House. The insult became "Reagan-loving fag-hater" and then "Bush-loving fag-hater." However, Albee has now decided to cut the presidential reference entirely. He feels, he says, that the line has become "too specific," now that most plays, movies and TV comedies contain Bush insults. (Lawson)

When he was writing the play, Albee had just read Elizabeth Kubler-Ross's book, *On Death and Dying*; it is likely that the character Elizabeth's name is, perhaps, an homage, and its plot a demonstration of Kubler-Ross's "stages of dying." The play's title refers to Harold Ross's remark that *The New Yorker* is "not . . . written for the little old lady from Dubuque," and, since that magazine is Albee's favorite, we can assume that the title is a sardonic one. Originally it was to be called "The Substitute Speaker" (*ASJ*, 184) a title that seems to suit *The Man Who Had Three Arms* far more literally.

The Man Who Had Three Arms

"I find it hard sometimes to distinguish between my self-disgust and my disgust with others," the main character, called Himself, tells us in act 2. And with that he seems to summarize the central problem of this, Albee's least successful play: it is not whether *The Man Who Had Three Arms* is an autobiographical diatribe, what Frank Rich called in his excoriating review "a temper tantrum in two acts," but rather whether that "disgust" overwhelms the play. Albee has defended the script, including it in volume 3 of *The Collected Plays* and thereby continuing its life (although he omitted other plays from the collection) and continuing the controversy. He calls it "one of my best plays . . . It is tough, outrageous, funny, and scalding, and it drove its major subject—critics and how they misuse their power, creating false gods as displays of their power and then, as arbitrarily, destroying them—into fits of apoplexy" (3:8).

Albee's disdain for theater critics (an animosity to which he gives gleeful vent in the tiny play *Knock! Knock! Who's There!?*) may be one of the play's issues, but it is difficult to see it as the play's "major subject," and only if we read it as the playwright's autobiographical revenge on the critical establishment does "critics and how they misuse their power" seem to be even a minor subject. The "major subject" seems to be a condemnation of society's adulation of its celebrities—people who are famous for being famous, a subject that would lend this play vivid relevance in today's culture of unearned fame. The hollowness of manufactured celebrity is represented in a scathing portrait of a man who fell for his own hype, and who was so greedy for easy wealth that he was gullible enough to believe his slimy agent's promises. By extension, then, the play is a denunciation of American society, where values of genuine worth and even manners have collapsed in failure—a denunciation heard frequently in Albee's plays.

The Man Who Had Three Arms "scalds" not only Albee's arch enemies, the critics, but also their coconspirators, the audiences. This humorless, sour play casts us as Himself's audience—his words are in the form of direct address—and our role is amplified by clues sprinkled liberally throughout the script, identifying us as small-town, middlebrow, easily shocked, sycophantic autograph hounds, people without taste or discrimination. One imagines the only way to escape this role, if one is actually sitting in the theater watching a performance, is to share the author's contempt. This elitist league of scorn would seem counterproductive for a play purportedly about the ethical failings of American society.

Himself faces the audience as an invited lecturer, telling the putative assembled crowd his "oh-so-sad-sad-story," a man whose fame is based on his having grown a third arm. When the arm disappears as inexplicably as it appeared, Himself's glamorous life disappears with it and he rails against the fate that having raised him up, brought him down. This could be, in our era of shallow, short-lived stardom, a fertile field for social criticism, since fame, which may be based on talent or accomplishment or deeds, is not identical to media-created celebrity. (Such constructs are not the product of "critics" but of tabloid journalists and paparazzi, surely a necessary distinction.) Any serious discussion of the difference between show business and dramatic art is erased by the play's crass, broad strokes.

If the arm is a metaphor for success—the kind of success Albee had early on in his career and then lost in his "middle period" as one play after another disappointed expectations—it is a flawed metaphor. The distinction between vanished fame and vanished talent is blurred by Himself, whose tone (depending, one imagines, on an actor's delivery) shifts between the contemptuous and the self-mocking:

> After we are done here, as you move into the lobby, you will find a table, a long one, with photographs, groups of photographs, booklets, a clinical case study, the coffee table volume, as well as my autobiography—illustrated, naturally! All for sale, all rare, all well worth the small price. And if you see me there, I beg you, please be gentle. I am not a freak. I am an average gentleman— easily injured . . . crushed! I am nothing more—or less—than a quiet man who, at one time, for a little, was possessed of . . . an extra arm. I no longer am. Please don't stare at me when we meet as if I were obscene, or deformed. I do not, I no longer bear arms. There is no appendage lurking underneath my jacket: it's gone. I waved it goodbye and it waved back. Gone. (3:150)

This is his introduction to his story, interspersed with earnest philosophical chitchat about how "I have never thought it was man's lot— his right—to be 'happy'" (3:150). He explains how the little bump on his back grew and grew into an arm and then shrunk away. Thus, the third arm would seem to represent talent—that extra something some people have that makes them able to do what most people cannot do, like write good plays. It is a psychological cliché that many artists are haunted by the fear that one day their talent will desert them, that they will wake up one morning and find they no longer can do what they once did. The dwindling of Himself's third arm would seem to be a self-lacerating metaphor for the state of Albee's career in 1982 (the year *The Man Who Had Three Arms* opened), with the flop of *The Lady from Dubuque* preceding it in 1980, followed by the flop of *Lolita* in 1981. Albee vigorously denies that the play is self-referential, as evidenced by his remarks to Stephen Bottoms in "Borrowed Time":

> I don't understand how anybody thought—how critics decided—that that play was about my career. Because I say, right in the middle of the play, "I didn't write fifteen string quartets, for Christ's sake, I didn't split the atom. I grew a fucking third arm. Where's the talent in

that?" How they would pretend it was about me, and that I'd lost my writing ability, is just *gratuitous*. (*SMM*, 173)

Despite Albee's claims "that the audience has a wonderful time during the two weeks of previews in New York: they were standing up cheering, and laughing all through it" (*SMM*, 172), it closed after sixteen performances. Even Mel Gussow's sympathetic biography acknowledges that the play is "lacking in humor" (*ASJ*, 326).

Himself's alcoholism produces an imagined license to abuse others; the playwright sketches a self-destructive impulse with what seems shocking candor, since Albee's abusive alcoholism was, before he stopped drinking, notorious. In one of the play's nastier scenes, Himself waves to a journalist he particularly despises: "Hello, dear! Be sure to put something in about the gin: attribute everything to that: 'The arm fell off because of the gin,' or something like that" (3:164). Prior to that, Himself argues that he is entitled to a glass of gin at the podium, while Woman, outraged, says, "Sir! You are addressing us!" Albee indulges in an egregious Friend of Dorothy moment, echoing the Judy Garland song "Over the Rainbow," when Himself replies, "Well, why can't I do it with a glass of gin in my hand?! If priests do it, why, oh why can't I?" This anticlerical attitude, echoing *Tiny Alice*, seems peculiarly irrelevant to this play, one of the many indulgent moments that seem, to use Albee's own word, *gratuitous*.

Finding the Sun

Despite the fact that Albee is gay, this one-act is his only play overtly about homosexual men, and for that reason one could wish it were more substantial. The pivot of the plot is that two men, Daniel and Benjamin, formerly lovers, are now married to women who do not like each other, for obvious if complicated reasons. The men seem to have married conventionally as a way of countering Daniel's assertion to his father, Henden, that his "nature" is both a "specialness" and a "disgrace." Unhappiness—mild and acute—is the result of such a "nature." Whether the characters' attitudes are the internalized results of social homophobia, or the results of each person's particular psychosexuality, this play offers little emotional insight and, surprisingly, no sociopolitical commentary.

If Daniel and Benjamin's relationship is the plot's engine, our *ciccarone* through the maze of the play's eight beach chairs and the eight bodies upon them is Fergus, a preternaturally inquisitive sixteen-year-old boy who comes to the beach with his mother, Edmee (this peculiar name suggests she is Albee's surrogate, i.e., *Ed* plus *me*, although this leads to silly conclusions). In scene 1, each of the four pairs of characters arrives, oblivious of the presence of the others; all wear bathing suits, carry similar "beach stuff," and each pair performs the same action—stretching in pleasure, and remarking to each other about "finding the sun." This first scene ends comically when all eight characters, having settled themselves on the beach, say, in unison, "Ahhhhhhhhh!" (3:200). In fact, each brief scene ends with a laugh line, except for the final one, although halfway through the twenty-one scenes, the comedy grows darker and the laughter more rueful or mocking.

The title's auditory pun on sun/son may echo Ibsen's famous final line in *Ghosts*, "Mother, give me the sun," spoken by Osvald to his mother, Mrs. Alving, as his brain collapses from inherited syphilis and his mother is faced with a terrible decision: whether to honor his last wish and administer a fatal dose of morphine or to save his life and thus condemn him to a vegetative state. In this grim play the sun is the symbolic curative to the gloomy Norwegian weather that represents all the cold, restrictive, joyless attitudes toward life Ibsen is indicting. Ibsen's drama about society's repressive and destructive restraints on sexuality, written a century before Albee wrote *Finding the Sun*, looks far bolder and far more enlightened.

The mother in Albee's play unwittingly condemns her son to death; he overhears Emdee's conversation with Gertrude and Hendon:

> You know what bothers me most about him, about Fergus—being so special, being so . . . bright, so beautiful and bright? That he'll turn out . . . less than he promises, I don't want to be around when his hair recedes or his body starts his way to fat; I don't want to see the expression in his eyes when he looks at his life and sees it's not going to be quite what it might have been. Tarnish! That's what I don't want to see . . . tarnish. (3:232–33)

We—and they—do not see Fergus again; the suggestion is that he has drowned himself, a preemptive strike, one imagines, the athlete dying young, suicide being one of the "options" open to young people, as Fergus points out. Edmee's shallow worry about her son's future—expressed entirely in superficialities of loss of good looks, of "tarnish," seems a caricature of gay preoccupations. Most mothers worry about their children's health and happiness, about their finding love and doing worthy work, not about their growing paunchy and going bald.

The mother-son relationship between Edmee and Fergus seems perverse; although Edmee says she worries about Fergus's Oedipal feelings ("given the provocation, Fergus would bed me in a moment," 3:214), it is her unacknowledged sexual fixation on her teenage son that is conspicuous enough to make a stranger curious. Gertrude asks, "What is he to you, or am I being nosy? [. . .] is he your son, your nephew, your ward your . . . lover?" (3:203). Edmee replies, "What he is to me is too much" (3:213). She admits that since her last husband dove off the rocks and drowned, their "attachment transcends the usual, the socially *admitted* usual," and this reveals Albee's naked interest in forcing his audience to admit that sexuality is more complex than the "socially admitted usual" (an impulse to *épater le bourgeois* that will be given far more serious expression in *The Goat or, Who Is Sylvia?*) Worth noting here is this bit of dialogue that seems to anticipate the later play:

> EDMEE. What *is* he to me? Who is Henden?
> GERTRUDE. Or, more to the point, who is *Sylvia?* (3:203)

Abigail, Benjamin's unhappy wife, tries and fails to drown herself. In scene 19, she wonders, "Why am I so cold all the time?" And raising "her hand to the sun" she says, "Why don't you just . . . go out? Burn out? Flare up, sizzle, crackle for a moment, and then . . . just . . . fade . . . bring the ice down on all of us? *I'm* ready; *I'm* cold enough. Go out! I dare you!" (3:238). At the moment when the sun goes "away," Benjamin childishly frets, "What if it were to . . . go out?" (3:242), all of which seems to echo not only Ibsen but also Albee's recurring dream about the end of the world (*SMM*, 61–62), a likely source for the imagery of these postapocalyptic plays, although he himself does not suggest the link (this dream is discussed further in the section of this book on *Box-Mao-Box*). *Finding the Sun* is a grim play—paradoxically made all the grimmer by being so warmly and brightly lit. The lighting directions Albee supplies in the headnotes specify "Bright sun; August, a New England day. Toward the end of the play, a lighting shift; until then, still sun," while for the setting he specifies "a beach in bright sun. Eight beach chairs—candy striped of or various colors," visually suggesting, as do the laugh lines early on, a far more festive atmosphere than will be the case.

Perhaps the most disappointing aspect of this play is its language. Albee's usually sharp ear seems to have failed him, and the dialogue often seesaws between extremes of crudity and pretentiousness. Abigail, who is twenty-three and American, says things like, "Damn your eyes!" and "It gives me the pip!" as though she were a character in an old English movie. Edmee goes on and on about "tristesse" (a favorite Albee stage direction): "I don't know what it is about the sea—the beach and the sea: they bring out in me a tristesse I feel no other place. It's not lugubrious sadness or a grief" (3:236). The convoluted, formal syntax makes her seem ludicrous—especially considering she is talking to a stranger on a beach. Daniel lapses into the sermonesque in conversation with his father: "*I* can't keep my hands from shaking, *or* shouting at you, dearest man, whom I love above all creatures on this earth" (3:235). How would actors convincingly deliver these lines? Mingled in with all this are breezy, pointless allusions to Wilde's *The Importance of Being Earnest.* Gertrude says, "Henden is my husband, my third; the other two I lost—not through carelessness, but time" (3:203) as well as the Shakespearean names—Gertrude, Cordelia—that seem to lead nowhere.

The play was commissioned by the University of Northern Colorado; its initial production was directed by Albee there, and was subsequently staged at University of California at Irvine. Albee explains in his "author's note" to the Dramatists Play Service script that *Finding the Sun*'s 1987 New York production was postponed when Tina Howe's play, *Coastal Disturbances,* coincidentally opened off-Broadway, another play with a beach setting and with what Albee called

a not dissimilar group of characters and—inevitably—some of the same general preoccupations.

Gut instinct told me that while the two plays were independent conceptions Miss Howe's had occupied the field—or the beach, to be more exact and, should mine be then presented some cloudy journalistic minds would deduce that the earlier play (mine) had been substantially influenced by the later one (Miss Howe's).

Life is tough enough these days without any of that nonsense, so I have postponed New York production of *Finding the Sun* for a while, at least until the sea air clears.

Finding the Sun finally opened in New York in 1993 when Signature Theatre presented a season of Albee plays.

Marriage Play

Marriage Play stands about equidistant in time between Albee's two more famous dramatic meditations on marriage, *Who's Afraid of Virginia Woolf?* (1962) and *The Goat* (2002). It opened in Vienna in 1987 and then for five years went unseen until its unsuccessful 1992 production under Albee's direction. Like so many of his plays, *Marriage Play* is about "a marriage of some duration and persistence between two heretofore quick and rational people" (3:254). Much later the wife tells her husband, "This is not our *first* marriage, friend; this is *marriage*" (3:304), and her line is crucial to Albee's view of the socially sanctified relationship: the point is in the enduring. In Albee's marriage plays, the issue is never divorce or breaking up, nor anything so sentimental as rediscovering love, but, simply, stamina, staying the course, being *married.*

Marriage Play is, on one level, a realistic portrait of a marriage. The relationship is signature Albee, played out between highly articulate, literate, intuitive people who are immensely fed up with each other's predictable shtick. The first stage direction, "Looks up from her book; fairly friendly" gives us the opening bell: "fairly friendly" is the best it is going to be, and it is downhill from there. Keep in mind, in contemplating this downhill metaphor, that their names are

Jack and Gillian, that is, Jack and Jill, and, like He and She of *Counting the Ways*, or Man and Woman of *The Play About the Baby*, they are a prototypical, if not actually archetypal, couple. The play's realism is amply supported by the set and costumes and props that fully ground the play in a "suburban home." The realism is further extended by the long, actor-challenging physical fight between them, which Albee hopes, according to his stage directions, will end in bloodied noses and lips. The look may be Ibsen, the atmosphere may be Strindberg, but *Marriage Play*, despite its debt to the nineteenth-century masters, is completely contemporary. In those earlier marriage plays (*A Doll's House*, *The Father*, *Dance of Death*) the struggle resolves: the ferocious battle between the sexes is won and lost. Here, Jack and Gillian battle to a draw, a fact that intensifies the claim to realism.

The dialogue is both realistic and absurdist. Often hilarious in its illustrations of miscommunication, Jack and Gillian's refrain runs something like, "What do you mean?" "What do you mean what do I mean?" Their frequent misunderstandings are, paradoxically, both inevitable and willful. Their conversation depends on timing and style, as, with the ease and venom of well-seasoned opponents, they have at each other: "Do you *try* to vex me?" "Only when you really want me to" (3:256). Although most of the ping-pong dialogue is in one-line ripostes, Jack has a central aria-like monologue. This recollection of his boyhood beauty, when he used to "glow," and his astonishingly unembarrassed account of how irresistible he was to dogs and to people reveal his profound vanity, explaining how he has husbanded this charismatic power ever since. This is a challenging scene for the actor playing Jack since he has to find some way not to sound either ridiculous or repulsive—or homosexual. Although most of the critical arguments that Albee's plays about heterosexuals are clandestinely about homosexuals seem forced and products of ax-grinding, there is a case to be made here; Jack's assertion that he was "too beautiful, too lucky, too this, too that" when he was fifteen is likely to strike the audience or reader as implausible from a middle-aged heterosexual man.

The absence of the article *The* in the title is noteworthy since it effectively shifts the meaning of the word *play* from "script" to "games"—and game-playing is a concept already elaborated in *Who's Afraid of Virginia Woolf?* (Get the Guests, Hump the Hostess, Peel the Label, etc.). One of the primary games here is linguistic, as it often is among Albee's articulate characters who, even in the middle of a life-altering argument, cannot help but admire an allusion or correct a misusage (a device used to great effect in *The Goat*). Central to their language games is "The Book of Days," her record of their sex life. As she reads passages, he identifies the literary stylistic influence—Hemingway, James, D. H. Lawrence—rather than react to the content. After a brief grammatical skirmish ("As who?" "Whom? *"Who"*) he says, "Try being you." Gillian replies, "I've *been* trying that. No good. It leads to . . . boredom, middle-age panic, dalliance, threats of departure. . . . I've tried that, sweetie; it doesn't work. I've tried it for thirty years" (3:272).

All their repetition ("You have done everything at least once too often," 3:260) is both realistic and stylized in this portrait of marriage, conveying both the tedium and the absurdity of life as it is lived. This seemingly endless redoing and rehashing is central to the domestic experience, just as it is central to the theatrical experience of performing a play—the merest reminder while we are watching that these lines have been spoken and these gestures made night after night. The thematic link between marriage and drama is established right at the start, as the first scene becomes a rehearsal: he enters saying, "I'm leaving you." After hilarious and intractable starts and stops, Jack is exasperated and decides to go out and come in again. This happens four times, with each "I'm leaving you" becoming sadder and funnier as he leaves and returns; the way the director blocks their action, mostly built into the dialogue, speaks the play's meaning, and that meaning we can only understand in retrospect once we have seen or read its stalemate-checkmate conclusion.

This exhausted paralysis reaches its fullest expression in that final scene, a realistic (and far nastier) version of the conclusion of Beckett's *Waiting for Godot*. There Gogo and Didi, who are emotionally as well as existentially connected, conclude,

VLADIMIR. Well? Shall we go?
ESTRAGON. Yes, let's go.
They do not move.
Curtain.

Jack and Gillian conclude,

> JACK. *(Finally; no emotion)* I'm leaving you.
> GILLIAN. *(Long silence; finally; no emotion)* Yes. I know.
> JACK: *(Long silence; little boy)* I am.
> GILLIAN. *(Long silence; gentle)* I know; I know you are.
> *(They sit, silence; no movement.)*

The similarities are obvious, especially the hopelessness, the impossibility of both "going" and "leaving," although the difference between the plural pronoun of "we" and the singular pronoun of "I" is crucial. Also crucial to Albee's portrayal of the male-female relationship is the husband's retreat to the petulant, helpless child role and the wife's yielding to the kind but authoritative maternal role.

The self-referential theatricality of their lives occurs over and over. When Gillian makes one of her two central speeches, "Have I gotten too old for you? [. . .] What*ever* is the matter? *(Waits)* No? Nothing?" (3:279), his response is "slow deliberate applause." And instead of being angry at his mockery, she smiles and curtsies. "Quite a performance," he tells her. The theatricality of their lives takes several other shapes as well; that they (and by extension, everyone) are always acting is made overt when, recalling their first date, he says, "There were four of us on that date . . . You; me; and the people we pretended to be." When she replies, "I think we probably should have married *them*—the two we were pretending to be," and, instantly another play is written in the air: "I wonder how it went with them. . . . Are they your stock happy couple, or was it a failure, prison, cancer and all the rest? Lucky in any event. At least nobody came home one day and said, 'Hi there! I'm leaving you'" (3:294).

The most remarkable dramatizing in this play comes through Gillian's reminiscence of a time spent in a Venetian hotel room; he insists they were in Venice only twice, while she narrates a third time, creating in the present of the play we are watching another play, where the revelation occurs as it would cinematically:

> GILLIAN. *(Happy)* Yes! I heard you in the downstairs hall, the desk; I heard you on the stairs and into the room. I pretended to be asleep; I heard you put your bag down; I heard your shirt rustle; I heard you unzip your trousers . . .
> JACK. *(Matter of fact)* It wasn't me.
> GILLIAN. I opened my eyes to your advancing form, and . . . no, it *wasn't* you, was it? (3:297)

It is all point of view, as everything is; Jack acknowledges this when he says of infidelity, "I can't stand it when it's you . . . When it's me I understand it and accept it" (3:300). It is interesting that Albee can manipulate our point of view while we are watching both characters, establishing the play's greater sympathy for Gillian. Even more theatrically complicated is their argument about listening (cf. Albee's *Listening*). In a spectacularly parsable accusation, Jack says: "You never listen . . . I suppose I mean you think you've heard all the resonances. You haven't, you know." And Gillian replies, "Your mind is always cocked for something else . . . I see you not listen" (3:301). Imagine the challenge to the actor who must listen and not listen, while *seeming* to listen and not listen so that we, too, can see it.

After all the sad struggles, they conclude on a reluctantly hopeful note when, with echoes of Willy Loman digging in his backyard in the middle of the night, Jack says, "It's time for the garden; it *would* be time for the garden." Gillian urges him to do what he has always done, despite his hopeless rage at the idea: "You put in a garden every year; you always have; it's hopeless every year—everything: the garden, going on, everything. You put in a garden; you do it every year. It is . . . what you do" (3:305). Note in the repetition another echo: in 1967 Albee adapted Giles Cooper's play and called it *Everything in the Garden*—another play about a feuding married couple—whose title Gillian seems to allude to. The play's final note is one of repetition—both the curse and the salvation of marriage. Even the dialogue repeats itself (not unlike the dialogue that concludes *Who's Afraid of Virginia Woolf?*) and their silences exhaustedly repeat themselves. The Beckettian echoes ("I can't go on, you must go on, I'll go on") in the final notes of *Marriage Play* reveal that, for Albee, repetition is both the torment and the comfort of life.

Three Tall Women

Albee's third Pulitzer Prize for Drama, awarded for *Three Tall Women* in 1994, commemorated his comeback to the forefront of American drama; it was that rare play which pleased audiences and critics and producers alike, an artistic and a commercial success. *Three Tall Women* is an intriguing play in a variety of ways, emotionally, psychologically, and biographically; it provides a sympathetic but not sentimental portrait of old age, a meditation on the passage of time, and an exploration of the essence of identity. It also provides insight into Albee's vexed relationship with his mother, another layer of interest. One might argue that the family resemblance extends far beyond the boundaries of this one script; these three women have much in common with many of Albee's female characters in many of the plays preceding *Three Tall Women*, and thus it can serve as a prism for much of the canon.

The play's subject is Albee's mother—his *adoptive* mother, a distinction he is always at pains to make. The mother-son relationship, elaborately chronicled in Gussow's biography, *A Singular Life*, as well as many other sources, was venomous: Frances Cotter Albee threw her son out of the family house when he was eighteen after having discovered his homosexual life and, later, cut him out of her sizable estate. The play's basis in autobiography is not speculation, but acknowledged by Albee. In the 1994 introduction to the Plume/Penguin edition, Albee rejects the motivation of revenge and declares his lack of interest in discovering or purging his own feelings about his mother:

> We had managed to make each other very unhappy over the years, but I was past all that, though I think she was not. I harbor no ill-will toward her; it is true I did not like her much, could not abide her prejudices, her loathings, her paranoias, but I did admire her pride, her sense of self. As she moved toward ninety, began rapidly failing both physically and mentally, I was touched by the survivor, the figure clinging to the wreckage only partly of her own making, refusing to go under.

He goes on to explain that he wanted "to write as objective a play as I could about a fictional character who resembled her in every way," remarkably certain he "would be able to be accurate without prejudice, objective without the distortive folly of 'interpretation.'" Whether his dead mother would have found her portrait a fair one is anybody's guess, but the play never feels vicious or vengeful, just as it does not feel maudlin or nostalgic. Psychologically, then, the play would seem to be a extraordinary achievement. But the work and not the man is the focus here.

As we watch or read act 1, the play's title seems to be merely descriptive—A, B, and C are the three tall women; then, at the beginning of act 2, we discover that the three tall women are really one tall woman at different stages of her life. This quiet and sly revelation begins with a pronoun when B, cataloging for C all the various ways one might die, mentions "the Chinese rug," which, B explains, "*We get* [. . .] at auction" (3:353; emphasis added). C could not know about this purchase since it had not yet happened in her twenty-six years—and the realization creeps up on us that all the characters are the same person at different stages of her life, viewed from different angles, what John Lahr in *The New Yorker* called "a kind of Cubist stage picture" (104). When the coup de théâtre happens it is dazzling: A seems to be dying in the bed upstage with an oxygen mask over her face, wearing what she was wearing in act 1. This turns out to be a mannequin, and the actor playing A sweeps in, in a "lovely, lavender dress," to nobody's surprise but ours. Thus what began as a character drama is revealed to be something far more profound: a dramatized rumination on the nature of personality and on the power of memory to reinvent reality; theater is the perfect medium in which to realize these ideas; it can make manifest the human interior drama.

At the end of the play, the three women join hands; the stage directions read, "A looks to C and B, puts her hand out, takes theirs." It is a gesture signifying self-integration, acceptance, the past uniting with the present—which is, of course, already past. The play shows us that personality is the accumulation of selves, and this final joining of hands is deeply moving because, if it is happening symbolically inside A's mind, she has come to peace with who she was and is. And since this gesture of joining hands comes at the conclusion of the play as well as at the conclusion of her life, it seems to be a theatrical gesture, too, exactly what the three actors would do, and do do, as they take their bows. Even A's last speech suggests the essential theatricality of self-awareness: "Sometimes when I wake up and start thinking about myself like that—like I was watching—I really get the feeling that I *am dead,* but going on at the same time" (3:384). This synopsizes the play we have just seen, and, further, includes us, as watchers of her watching herself, inviting the audience to identify with her, as any substantial play must invite identification between its audience and characters, thus allowing us to experience the emotional gratification of coming to terms, feeling psychologically whole and sound. In the last moments of the play, A says of the end of life, "None of that 'further shore' nonsense, but to the point where you *can* think about yourself in the third person without being crazy" (3:384), and at that point the character has merged with the play that contains her, and the audience with the play, in a solemn and liberating moment where all three elements become interwoven and, most important, interdependent.

The three female characters are developed to various degrees: act 1's C, the emissary from A's lawyer's office (it is unclear whether she is a lawyer herself) is the least successfully drawn. Her youth gives her confidence and a sense of entitlement to the world; she is unlikable and self-important, someone who feels the weight of the advantages of the prestigious legal firm behind her as well as her personal beauty and, of course, her height. She seems too naive about life and especially old age—it is as though she has never even noticed, in the world around her, the infirmities and indignities of old age or even peeked at her own mortality. As a woman incapable of imagining her own future, she represents Albee's frequently revisited notion of callow youth: she is unthinkingly convinced that her own health and beauty are permanent and that the best is yet to come. Further, on a realistic level, it is hard to imagine that a delegate from the law firm to the home of a long-standing client would be so rude, so inappropriate in her way of speaking to a very wealthy very old woman, despite what must be A's reputation as "difficult." In act 2, C continues to be shallow and irritating—plausible characteristics for A as a young woman in another era, although there is no depth to the shallowness, which is to say she is an underdeveloped character as well as an underdeveloped person. Perhaps, as this is a portrait of Albee's mother before he could have known her, C is thus a mere assumption, although the opposite is arguable: since she is purely fictionalized, Albee had no real constraints in inventing the character.

It is in middle age that the tripartite female character becomes interesting. B, who is A's caretaker in act 1, is ironical, witty, and patient with A if not with C. B, who, at fifty-two, is twice C's age, is the only character who is not unhappy or struggling against her position in life; she seems to feel no resentment about the often revolting tasks that are part of her job in act 1. Near the end of act 2 she says, "The happiest time? Now; now . . . always. This must be the happiest time; half of being adult done, the rest ahead of me. Old enough to be a *little* wise, past being really *dumb*." B relishes her "three-hundred-and-sixty-degree view," although her "Wow! What a view!" (3:383) strikes a somewhat Pollyannaish note. Albee himself must have felt he had such a view in order to create this tripartite portrait; in fact, Albee was in his mid-sixties when he wrote *Three Tall Women*.

A is, of course, the most fully developed character—literally and figuratively—since she is not only the play's focus, but also the oldest of the three tall women, thus having accumulated more experience and more selfhood; she has also lost selfhood through the erosions of time. On the play's realistic level, A's random reminiscences as her mind wanders provide the backstory of a life of privilege and self-indulgence as well as of terrible betrayals: her sister who was her best friend became a burdensome drunk, her husband became a womanizer and then an invalid requiring dreadful care, her mother became her enemy, and gives us another glimpse of grotesque old age: "I'm helpless, she . . . she screamed; I hate you! She stank; her room stank; she stank; I hate you, she screamed at me" (3:351), Her son "went away, took his life and one bag and went off" (3:370). A is offensive in many ways: she is a racist, a snob, and a paranoid. Domineering and pitiable, sexual and repressed, petulant and funny, nasty and wry, A is fascinating rather than likable.

Each of the three women has her time-of-life bias, and each believes her moment is the best—a remarkably positive inspection of the stages of life. There is no Jaques-like lamentation here ("Sans teeth, sans eyes . . .") despite the many physical and emotional losses (bones, friends) that have been recounted. And if C is optimistic because the future awaits her, and B is ironically cheerful about being halfway in life's journey, A finds consolation for the trials of old age in the very fact of nearing death. Her last speech is deeply moving and deeply Beckettian (Albee's debt to Beckett is often revealed in his plays' most thoughtful moments):

> (Shakes her head; chuckles; to B and C) You're both such children. The happiest moment of all? Really? The happiest moment? (To the audience now) Coming to the end of it, I think, when all the waves cause the greatest woes to subside, leaving breathing space, time to concentrate on the greatest woe of all—that blessed one— the end of it. (3:383–84)

Although A's philosophical speculations are more good-humored than most of Beckett's characters' speculations, Three Tall Women does bear a striking resemblance to Beckett's Rockaby, written in 1980. In this late, austere play, a woman (called only "W") sits in a rocking chair, reviewing her life and remembering her mother's death, which, wearing her mother's "best black," she may replicate in the course of the play. W speaks onstage, although most of the language of the play belongs to Voice, the actor's recorded voice-over, the woman's internal dialogue between past and present, between self and soul. The refrain in this stage poem is this:

till in the end
close of a long day
to herself
whom else
time she stopped
time she stopped

This last line is spoken by both the woman and Voice together, an aural version of the handholding gesture that concludes *Three Tall Women*. In both plays, the goal is to be done with it, and both A and W are ready to relinquish, with relief, their hold on life, as, in both plays, the internal generations of self merge. Both plays externalize the women's internal voices, dramatizing the passage of time and the vagaries of memory. In each, there is the significant chair, as well as the clothes, the mother, and the jewels, all creating a setting for female loneliness, regret, sadness, and the profound longing for what A calls, in *Three Tall Women*, "the end of it."

Beckett's characters often long for death—for silence, for cessation—so the similarities extend beyond this one comparison. In *Endgame*, Clov expresses A's thoughts on dying: "Then one day, suddenly, it ends, it changes. I don't understand that either. I ask the words that remain—sleeping, waking, morning, evening. They have nothing to say. *(Pause)* . . . When I fall I'll weep for happiness." In Beckett's *That Time*, where the characters are also named A, B, and C, all being voices belonging to the one character we actually see onstage but coming from three different theatrical locations, from each side and above. C's is the last we hear: "not a sound only what was it it said come and gone was that it something like that come and gone come and gone no one come and gone in no time gone in no time" (235).

In a talk to a meeting of Beckett scholars in December 2004,

Albee said that it was "nonsense" to characterize Beckett as an avant-garde playwright: "If the plays were set in a living room instead of a blasted heath, no one would have any trouble with them." Albee seems to have done exactly that: set his plays in a living room. Albee's most incisive observation on Beckett's genius may be in citing Beckett's line, "out there in the dark vast," noting that a lesser playwright would have said "vast dark." It is that dark vast that A has entered, although Albee his lit it beautifully for us in *Three Tall Women*.

The play's fourth character is an easily overlooked but important one. The son's role—by logical assumption Albee's self-portrait—is most remarkable for its silence; he has written no lines for himself. But since this is the boy his mother remembers when he left home (not the age he would have been by the time his mother was ninety-one), the character can exist only as a memory, a wish, an imagining of his mother's dying mind in act 2 as she, in effect, forces the young man to act out the grief she longs to make him feel. Albee remarked that the son's entrance came as a "complete surprise" to him. "I remember stopping and saying, 'Well isn't *that* interesting? How did you ever figure *that* out?'" ("Yes Is Better Than No," 38). Consider this character in light of Eugene O'Neill's self-portrait in his autobiographical play about his mother, *Long Day's Journey Into Night*; it is Edmond, of course, who is the playwright's surrogate, the poetic, tubercular young man, but most telling is that O'Neill gives the baby, whose death in some way began that family's terrible downhill journey, his own name, Eugene. Another lost child in another play about a baby.

Fragments

In 2002 at the Last Frontier Theatre Conference in Valdez, Alaska, which Albee had then overseen every June for ten years, each of the famous playwrights who were attending (including August Wilson, John Guare, and Jack Gelber) performed in a fully staged scene from one of his own plays. Albee chose to perform a scene from *Fragments*, sitting on a stool, facing the audience; this *is*, of course, "fully staged" for this script, which requires nothing more than sitting surfaces for eight actors and space for them to move around in from time to time. The significant alteration on this occasion of his performance was that he was alone with the audience; the seven other characters had vanished. He took for this performance the only extended monologue in the work, Man 1's speech at the start of act 2. It was a fierce and riveting performance, one of impressive power and precision.

The author's note preceding the script in volume 3 of *Collected Plays* reveals Albee's aggravation at the critical reception of this play:

> While *Fragments* is a play—looks like a play, sounds like a play, acts like a play—an unnerving number of critics (not audiences, I hasten to add) have declared that it isn't a play as they understand the term, and, therefore, it can't *be* one.

> While the problem *is*, I think theirs—the critics'—I have decided to call the piece a sit-around and let the critics figure out what *that* means. Certainly, anyone who decides to mount *Fragments* will not be accused of not doing a "play." (While they might be criticized for mounting a "sit-around," there are only so many of the world's problems I can solve.) (3:386)

Albee has frequently experimented with structure. And his plays have often lived to prove their critics wrong; an obvious case in point is the 1965 panning of *Tiny Alice* by the New York establishment, which then raved about the revival in 2000. However odd *Fragments* may be, this piece, thematically, occupies familiar Albee territory: sex, death, and the loneliness of the isolated individual. Its title suggests that people in any given group (and by extension, one imagines, any given society) feel themselves and expose themselves to be parts or fragments of the whole. Their wish to reveal themselves, to make some intimate connection with others, may be the motivating force behind their speeches; pulling against that notion is the announcement at the beginning of act 1 that they are in a play by Edward Albee. Man 4 tells the others (and the audience) "Edward Albee, who wrote this play, wanted you to know about this charity auction—a sort of celebrity auction he was asked to participate in," after which follows a not very entertaining but very long account of plastic eggs decorated for auction and which celebrities' eggs garnered the highest bids. This would seem to establish these characters in some Pirandellian no-man's-land: characters who know they are characters, rather than characters who think they are people.

The four men and four women are of specifically different ages; there is one African American man included as, perhaps, a way of extending the range of reactions and interactions beyond the sociopolitical triggers of generation and gender, although neither race nor generation nor gender seems to be the focus of the play. Whether there *is* a focus is the question; it could be argued that the very lack of center—the absence of any clear development of character or of narrative line—*is* the point, that *Fragments* illustrates fragmentariness by these deliberate lacks.

Albee explains it this way: "*Fragments* lacks plot in any estab-

Edward Albee reading from *Fragments*, Last Frontier Theatre Conference, Valdez, Alaska, 2002. (Photograph by Dawson Moore.)

lished sense; there is no clear dilemma and resolution—no 'story.'
. . . The piece proceeds as a piece of music does—accumulating, accumulating, following its own logic. Its effectiveness, its coherence reside in what we have experienced from the totality of it. *Fragments* is also a very simple, straightforward piece—on its own terms, of course" ("Edward Albee"). Before changing *Fragments'* subtitle to *A Sit-Around,* Albee subtitled it "A Concerto Grosso," a Renaissance musical style in which each instrument takes a solo. This is one of several of Albee's attempts to make drama approach the condition of music, suggesting the vital importance of timing in the performance of an Albee play and the interplay of voices as if they were instruments.

"Doing proverbs"—the first section of the script—requires each actor to recite a proverb and the others to comment on it; presumably this is a way to establish each character's attitudes and preoccupations, although since the proverbs are assigned to them, they are sometimes puzzled by what they have just read aloud; when Woman 4 reads, "Save something for the man who rides on the white horse," Man 2 asks, "What does that mean?" and she replies, "I have no idea" (3:390). The proverbs range from the familiar, like Benjamin Franklin's "Three may keep a secret if two of them are dead," to the totally unintelligible, "Dunder do gally the beans," which, after a mystified silence, provokes Woman 4 to say, "Yes that's the best one," and Man 2 to repeat his earlier proverb, "We have the greatest faith in things we don't understand?" (3:392). Research reveals this proverb to come from Somerset and, according to William Carew Hazlitt's *English Proverbs and Proverbial Phrases Collected from the Most Authentic Sources,* it means "Beans shoot up fast after thunderstorms." How—or if—this notion will develop in the course of *Fragments* creates a tantalizing prospect.

Eventually personalities emerge:

Woman 1, at twenty-five, is the youngest of the female group; she is also the silliest—perhaps reinforcing Albee's increasingly noticeable view of youth as callow. She is eager to be hopeful, easily shocked by Man 1's sexual asides, keen to hear the outcome of the celebrity story, crazy about musicals; she talks to plants, and her long story is about her cat and a possible mix-up about cremated ashes, although nobody seems to see the obvious flaw in the story: a human being would produce a far larger quantity of ashes than a cat.

Woman 2 is thirty years old, and tells a grotesque dog story, the companion piece to Woman 1's cat story. Again the plot involves a beloved pet's death and burial—made difficult by a frozen tail that won't fit into the dug grave. She goes on, at great length, in act 2 to bore us with an article about the psychological sources of nicknames.

Woman 3 describes her annual medical examination; she relates each unnecessary detail (every unbuttoning and buttoning) and reveals that the doctor discovered she was "pigeon-nippled." In act 2 she declares herself to be "a student 'of our times,'" and tells a story of a dinner party in which the celebrity draw was an actress so ancient as to be oblivious to what was going on around her. Her interest here seems to be sociological rather than human, and she shows no sympathy for the pathos of the described scene. Woman 3's anecdote about a kleptomaniacal schoolteacher is overrun by Man 3's story about his father, who was arrested after years of compulsive shoplifting.

Woman 4, sixty-five, is, like Man 4 ("fifty-five to sixty-five"), the most interesting of the group; they are closer than any of the other characters to Albee's own age at the time of writing. Woman 4's reminiscences are about things that have vanished through time, like knife-grinders.

Man 2, who is thirty and African American, is the rational skeptic, irritated by others' tolerance for the mystical, faux or otherwise; he refuses to accept what he sees as fake wisdom. His poem about removing your head and tossing it in the air provokes Woman 1 (not the best judge of poetic excellence) to say, "It's so . . . so sophisticated, so . . . subtle!" His prickly response (although Albee states he is "wryly amused") is to assume her remark is a racial slur: "What were you expecting . . . Vachel Lindsay's *The Congo*, for Christ's sake? I suppose I could have done some tap with it" (3:395).

Man 3, forty-five, narrates a bizarre dream he had, describing what sounds like a parody of this play: people move around silently, slowly, and then repeat it all. He concludes with a tossed-off line, the only genuinely funny line in the entire script: "Some nights your sleeping self just . . . moves into the *avant garde*, I suppose" (3:406). It is worth noting that when Man 3 talks about his problem with his sense of self, demonstrated by his problem with his reflection in the mirror, he describes the problem as "me, myself and I." Albee told me (winter 2005) that "Me, Myself and I" is the planned title of the play he is currently working on about identical twins.

Man 4, fifty-five to sixty-five, seems to be Albee's representative since he began with Albee's charity-event story. He confesses in act 2 that he feels he has missed being middle-aged, and gone directly from "feeling young—youngish [. . .] straight into old age" (3:453). Man 4's musings about the awareness of death are distinctly reminiscent of the way that subject is discussed by various characters in earlier Albee plays. The conclusion he comes to is, "While we may not be responsible for everything that *does* happen to us, we certainly are for everything that *doesn't*; that since we're conscious, we have to be aware of both the awful futility of it and the amazing wonder. Participate, I suppose" (3:456). This warning sounds familiar; Albee frequently returns to the dangers of safety. Man 3 responds to this with "some sarcasm," "Let me write this down." Man 4 seems impervious to his sarcasm.

I have saved Man 1 for last since not only does he have the largest part, but also because Albee chose to perform him. At twenty he is the youngest of the entire group, and he is also the most aggressive and the most sexual. He has fully assimilated what he takes to be proof of his desirability: "People want me; people have *always* wanted me. [. . .] People tried to kidnap me, to steal me out of my carriage, come in windows in the dead of night, stand by my crib and breathe there in the dark, just staring at me" (3:431). Gussow's biography reports that Albee has had, since childhood, the fear of being kidnapped, and cites this section of *Fragments*, specifically, adding that "every night before going to bed, Albee instinctively checks all doors and windows to make sure they are locked. [This strikes me as dubious evidence: What New Yorker is *not* lock-conscious?] He never says goodnight, but, as he did so many years ago with his nanny, he says, for luck, 'See you in the morning'" (*ASJ*, 348). Psychologists could argue that this fear of kidnapping springs from being an unhappily adopted child, but what seems most dramatically interesting here is that Man 1 does not sound fearful but rather proud, not unlike the vain husband in *Marriage Play* who recalls that he used to "glow." He relates his story: as the boy toy of an older man, another man tries to hire him, the then fifteen-year-old boy, to rape his daughter and then report to him about it; the story is shocking in its violence as well as its perversion. The boy falls in love with the girl's innocence and then has to escape her father's rage when he discovers he has been duped. Man 1's brush with something clean and sweet has lingered with him through what we gather is his sordid life. Note, too, that others in the group immediately attack him at the conclusion of his long set piece, their mockery led by Woman 1, joined by Man 2; the older characters admonish them feebly with, "That's not very nice, now" until Man 2 launches into a diatribe about Ralph Ellison and being black and the condition of not only not being wanted, but of not being seen.

The play concludes—or at least ends—with a reprise of the proverbs, with Man 1 repeating the ludicrous, "Dunder do gally the beans" and Man 4 adding (as the audience well might), "Yes, exactly."

The Play About the Baby

In many ways, Harold Pinter is to British drama what Albee is to American, although their positions are so major and international that the national designations may be merely descriptions of vernacular and locale. The similarities extend from their early fierce domestic dramas, the most prominent examples being *The Homecoming* and *Who's Afraid of Virginia Woolf?*, to their left-leaning social agendas. But while Pinter's later plays have become more overtly political in content and more austere in style, Albee's have become more probingly philosophical, while, stylistically, his dialogue has become simultaneously more caustic and more hilarious; he is one of the few playwrights who can have an entire audience laughing and then suddenly wipe the smiles off faces by revealing the shocking, appalling underside of a comic situation or witty remark. Thus Pinter's comment about Albee (on the occasion of the opening of *The Goat* in London) is expectably apt: "I think what is one of the most pronounced ingredients in his work is mischief" (Edemariam).

"Mischief" is an intriguing word to choose, suggesting both antic playfulness and potentially disproportionate harm. Mischief is central to *The Play About the Baby*, both in content and in style: it is a play about mischief and about mischief-makers, written by an accomplished mischief-maker. Consider the early lines from *Oth-*

ello, where the Duke seems to announce the dramatic events to come:

> To mourn a mischief that is past and gone
> Is the next way to draw new mischief on.
> What cannot be preserv'd when fortune takes
> Patience her injury a mockery makes.
> The robb'd that smiles steals something from the thief;
> He robs himself that spends a bootless grief.
>
> (1.3.204–9)

The plot of *The Play About the Baby* seems to toy with this Shakespearean advice; Boy and Girl, living in erotic Edenic joy, give birth to a baby in the first moments of the play. Enter Man and Woman, who have come to take away the baby by convincing the two young people that the child never existed. At first, Boy and Girl suffer and protest, but finally see that their grief is "bootless." Although their surrender to circumstances seems to have more denial and confusion in it than wisdom and patience, their being reconciled to the circumstances, to the vagaries of "fortune," creates the same effect.

Man and Woman are far more major and interesting characters than Boy and Girl; Albee has always had a certain measure of contempt for callow youth. Their innocence and its necessary loss is the play's plot and theme. The characters' attitudes, like their generic names, are thumbnail sketches, stages of life determined by gender and age, and not by personality. Thus character, as we usually mean the term in drama, is absent: they are types, lacking individuality.

Boy is immature and self-absorbed, driven by testosterone; we learn all there is to know about him from the first moments of the play when he asks Girl if the delivery "hurt a lot" and then begins a long tale about his memory of the pain caused by a gang of boys who broke his arm to punish him when he called the guards to report their trying to sneak into the "Hopeless Mothers" concert. What is telling is that Girl sees immediately the consequences of his act, while he seems still naively indignant that they would try to avoid paying for tickets at a benefit (the charity being "Mother's Milk") and would

pretend "no hard feelings," offering to shake his hand and then crack-
ing his arm. The whole event is, by Boy's own analysis, a result of his
endorphin high, having just come from the gym, combined with his
enchantment with his own forearms. He speaks most of his lines
after Girl has left with the sleeping baby—he never notices his audience is gone—and when she returns she comforts him as she does the
baby, offering him her breast and saying "Shhhhh," while he continues to whine his story, even when the words become "mumbled
as he fastens his mouth on her breast" (3:465). His next appearance
finds him wiping his mouth, licking his lips, and smiling, declaring
to Woman that he has just been "mountain climbing," an image that
eludes her, perhaps because it is such a adolescently crude metaphor
that she assumes he is speaking literally. Despite his own trusting
nature, he is scornful of Girl's gullibility in believing the fortune-
telling gypsy. But since the gypsy becomes the voice of those who
would steal the baby, Girl's fears are well founded, and Boy's vow,
"I'll guard you. I'll guard the baby" (3:488), is mere youthful bravado,
based on his stereotypical understanding of his gender role and on his
lack of awareness of the inevitable losses life brings.

Gender roles inform the play: it is not insignificant that Girl is
the only one of the four characters who has no long speech; although
she seems to understand more than Boy, she is relegated to a young
version of Woman, who fulfills a very retrograde and clichéd notion
of the female. As Woman explains in her introductory address to the
audience, "The man indicated me as he exited, said 'Woman' and
exited. Remember? That's why I'm here—to be with him. To help
. . . him; to assist him" (3:472). This Eve-like helpmeet, in a play that
seems to be Albee's version of Genesis, casts the playwright as God;
the question is whether The Play About the Baby is a revisionist creation myth or a satire of patriarchal society.

Man delivers a series of anecdotal lectures on such subjects as the
nature of loss, the instability of reality, and the unreliability of memory. But these are delivered to the audience, not to Boy and Girl, and
unless we are as radically inexperienced and uninitiated as Boy and
Girl are, the play begins to sound like a freshman course, Life 101.
The intended effect seems to be, with much winking and nudging,

that the audience respond with knowing chuckles of "how true, how true." When Man discourses on the underrated/underdeveloped tactile sense, he illustrates his point with a sculpture exhibition for the blind in London where visitors were encouraged to touch the art. Just as he pretends to be blind, both at the exhibition and bumping into the chairs onstage, so, later, Woman will pretend to use sign language, another defiantly politically incorrect moment. The visual and the tactile merge in Woman's "art" story, in which, as a young woman, braless in Europe, wearing "delicious silk, an unlined silk, smooth against my nipples," she met a painter who found her outfit "very Gainsborough, or perhaps Watteau" (3:489). Her story of their love affair, which Man disbelieves and encourages us to hear as a fabrication, is a "turn" delivered to applause and with a curtsey; this is youth remembered as performance rather than experience.

After his riff on "youngsmell" (Man keeps smelling his fingers with much eyebrow waggling), he recounts an experience of memory failure at a cocktail party when he introduced two friends to a "the older woman standing next to me . . . I knew she was familiar, but I couldn't, for the life of me, remember who she was." It was his mother, and that moment was "the worst—so far!" (3:467). He concludes the story with an attempt at self-consolation: "*Nobody* dies from not being remembered," although he has apparently forgotten that his mother died three years after this cocktail party episode. (In his brief introduction to *A Delicate Balance* in *Collected Plays*, Albee, writing about his own failing memory, tells us, "Once I looked straight at my mother and couldn't figure out who she was," 2:13.) After more sniffing of fingers, Man concludes with, "Pay attention to this, what's true and what isn't is a tricky business, no? What's real and what isn't? Tricky. Do you follow? Yes? No? Good. *(Shrugs)* Whichever" (3:468). This reprise of an idea demonstrated—rather than lectured on—with far more complexity in *Who's Afraid of Virginia Woolf?* seems both vulgar in its disdain for the audience's level of sophistication and crass in its presentation.

This allusion to the theater as a metaphor for life—a fundamental idea in *Who's Afraid of Virginia Woolf?* as George and Martha argue about illusion and reality—is less engaging and charming than Man seems to think it is. The play makes almost no attempt to sustain the theatrical illusion and teases the audience with endless deconstructions of its "reality." The challenge to reality and to our perception of it is distilled in the important shift that takes place at the end of act 1:

> MAN. *(Cheerless smile)* What do we *want.* Well, it's really very simple. We've come to take the baby. *(Silence)*
> BOY. What do you mean!?
> MAN. *(Flat)* We've come to take the baby. *(Shorter silence)*

After a few more exchanges like this, Girl rushes onstage.

> GIRL. *(Reenters from left; hysterical)* WHERE'S THE BABY?! WHAT HAVE YOU DONE WITH THE BABY?! *(Silence)*
> MAN. *What* baby? *(Silence)*
> WOMAN. Yes; *what* baby? *(Tableau)* (3:495–96)

Thus Man's self-consciously cute opening lines in act 2 undergo a jarring tonal shift; he hurries the audience in from intermission, hectors the smokers about the dangers thereof, and rehashes all the obvious complaints about the size of ladies' restrooms; and then, with another surprising shift, he rails at the fraudulence of the belief of sentimental movies that "good things happen to good people," an objection too sophomoric to take seriously. Then his speech culminates in a surprising moment of profundity:

> I know it can never happen in what they call "real life"? Good things to good people and happy endings? That it's all . . . fantasy? [. . .] If I saw it *really* happening—all good things to all good people?— would I turn away in horror? Yes, probably, because it could all . . . stop, could go away, be a single instant of glory, desperately cruel. We can't take glory because it shows us the abyss. (3:498)

A similar thought is expressed in *The Goat,* when Stevie, Martin's wife, gently mocks his state of mind on his fiftieth birthday: "The old foreboding? The sense that everything going right is a sure sign that everything's going wrong, of all the awful to come? All that?" If this, like the insupportable glimpse of glory Man speaks of, is a way of defining tragedy, then Man's and Woman's task is to initiate Boy and Girl into their tragic view of life, what Albee offers as "realistic," a vision of life that is deeply pessimistic. Albee's relish in disabusing youth of its optimism, which he places in Man's and Woman's mouths, seems to argue that being cruel is a kindness. This is the justification Man provides:

> If you have no wounds how can you know if you're alive? If you have no scar how do you know who you are? Have been? [. . .] If you don't have the wound of a broken heart, how can you know you're alive? If you have no broken heart, how do you know who you are? Have been? Can ever be? (3:509)

Man and Woman continue with vicious vaudevillian attacks to demolish Boy's and Girl's naive love and hopefulness; the suggestion at this juncture is that Man and Woman are Boy and Girl's future selves (perhaps a variant of the temporal device of *Three Tall Women*), and finally Man advises the younger pair: "No; the question is not who I think I am, but who I cannot be [. . .] I've lived long enough to understand that *that* is the most important question. Keep it in mind as you go on through it—both of you: what we cannot do; who we cannot be" (3:521). Thus selfhood is defined by lack, by the negative, by loss gained through the passage of time.

Time, is, of course, the real subject of the play—as it is in many of Albee's plays—reinforced by Man's and Woman's persistent remark, "Time's up." This is the end of the time of innocence, underscored by the cloying refrain, "Oh what a wangled teb we weave," a remixed version of Sir Walter Scott's "Oh what a tangled web we weave when first we practice to deceive" (a self-consciously cute locution heard earlier from the wife in *Marriage Play*). The implication of the quotation is obvious: the danger of deception is self-deception. The concluding lines of the play, when Boy and Girl tell each other they hear the baby crying, may be their self-deception—as Boy says, they are too young for "terrible things happening," and have therefore reinvented reality to meet the need. Alternatively, we may understand that Boy and Girl refuse to be deceived into the erasure of their grief, that Man and Woman's insistence that there was no baby cannot be accepted. Man and Woman function as the agents of the passing of time, of Boy's and Girl's becoming less innocent, less sympathetic, less emotionally vulnerable. Thus they are both the proof of and the refutation of the lesson of the play: only wounds shape us, only loss defines us. The ambiguity of the concluding scene is akin to the vaudevillian bit Man and Woman stage with "the old blanket trick," revealing that there is no baby wrapped in the blanket, just as there is no ambiguity wrapped in the play.

The Play About the Baby divides both audiences and critics radically: some find it pretentious, self-parodic, and tedious, while others find it profound, amusing, and disturbing. The play is Albee at his most acrid and acidic. The title is, of course, jokey, engendering "Who's on first?" conversations; it also seems to be self-referential, since it could be the subtitle of his most famous play, *Who's Afraid of Virginia Woolf?* As I have discussed elsewhere in this volume, Albee's plays are filled with disappearing, invisible, imaginary, and destroyed children. It is odd that, having examined with such subtlety and psychological delicacy the issues of parental longing and regret, he would offer such a blatant reprise late in his career. Man seems to sum up his author's problem: "Well, first we *invent*, and then we *re*invent" (3:468).

The Goat or, Who Is Sylvia?

The Goat is an audience-shocking play about a happy family; Martin, a world-famous architect, is married to Stevie, a loving, clever woman; Billy is their sweet, smart teenage son. Martin, it is revealed, is having a passionate love affair with a goat named Sylvia. He confides his outrageous secret to his friend Ross, who then feels obliged to tell Stevie, bringing their idyllic family life crashing down in ruins.

In a televised interview on the occasion of *The Goat*'s 2002 Tony nomination for Best Play (an award it won), Albee told Charlie Rose that he wants this play to make people "imagine what they cannot conceive of imagining, to imagine how they would feel if they were in this situation, to learn something about the nature of love, of tolerance, and consciousness." During that same television interview, Mercedes Rhuel, who played Stevie in the original New York production, said she thought *The Goat* was about the profound loneliness of being un-understood by the people we love most. Bill Pullman, who played Martin in that production, said the play was about having any passion others saw as unacceptable; he offered as an example his decision to become an actor, based on a passion for theater he said he that he could not, would not be dissuaded from.

Christopher Caldwell quotes the late, great literary critic Lionel

Trilling on Nabokov's *Lolita:* it is "not about sex, it's about love," the kind of passion involving suffering and doom. In contemporary art, Trilling adds, "no passion can shock, no amatory choice is despised, no one is doomed. Lovers as jealous as Othello or as thwarted by snobbery as Romeo and Juliet would be implausible. To create a protagonist doomed by passion, you must seek the only taboo left standing: pedophilia." Trilling goes on to declare that *Lolita* is a "a bid to rescue love from the forces of health—marriage on the one hand and psychiatry on the other—in order to reclaim it for suffering and for art." But perhaps by now pedophilia has also been so discussed, legislated, and psychiatrically exempted that Albee has been forced to go even further afield than Nabokov to find a taboo still standing.

It is worth remembering here that Albee adapted Nabokov's novel for the stage twenty-one years before he wrote *The Goat;* that earlier play, *Lolita,* contains this exchange:

> HH [Humbert Humbert]. We all know "rut." Rut, that purely physical passion, where "hello" from the object produces an erection, and "how are you?" an orgasm. We all know about that, and we all know about the pure and hopeless love—that which would perish if life were pumped into it. There is, as well [. . .] though most often in fiction, the doomed passion of the very great, the . . . powerful, the beloved of the public—the Duchess of Windsor and Joe DiMaggio: Edward the Eighth and everybody's Marilyn, that sort of thing. Then . . . then there are the loves that dare not speak their names. These are usually perfectly rational relationships between people of the same sex, of different colors and now and again with other animals.
>
> ACG [A Certain Gentleman, who serves as Albee/Nabokov surrogate]. Forgive me; I must interrupt you. A perfectly rational relationship with another animal?
>
> HH. It is theoretically possible. *(To the audience)* I can conceive of conceiving—of such a relationship: a man and his ewe; a lady and her tiger; all things are possible. And, most things are ultimately permissible in this ultimately permissive society of ours—most things but not all. [. . .] I have—here comes that word again—I have fallen in love, with a girl named Lolita; Lo-lee-ta. [. . .] she is younger than you might expect one to be who is the object of the

. . . breathtaking ardor of one who is thirty-eight years old. Lolita, after all, is . . . eleven. (3:14–15)

In his essay "About This Goat," Albee writes, "The play [*The Goat*] is about love, and loss, the limits of our tolerance and who, indeed, we really are." He continues, "The play is about what it is about, and all I ask of an audience is that they leave their prejudices in the cloakroom and view the play objectively and later—at home— imagine themselves in the predicament the play examines" (*SMM*, 262–63). There is a fleeting precursor to this taboo subject: in *The Man Who Had Three Arms* (1982), we hear about "a noted zoologist, Dr. Henry Speedthrift Tomlinson" who fell to his death "into an Andean crevasse"; on the decomposed body was a locket containing "two photographs, one of the late doctor himself, and the other of . . . *(Disbelief)* a large pig" (3:143).

The play's title provides multiple meanings. Albee told Charlie Rose that *The Goat* referred to both the real animal and the sense of the word that suggests the butt of a joke, "the goat." But never trust a playwright to give it all away, or even, necessarily, to know how much meaning he has achieved by an intuitive leap of creativity. The title offers the obvious possibility of "the scapegoat" as we use the word colloquially: the one selected conveniently and arbitrarily to take the blame; in the plot of the play, the goat is wholly innocent, victimized by Martin's obsessive love and by Stevie's murderous revenge. The idea of the scapegoat comes from ancient Hebraic ritual, part of the ceremonies of Yom Kippur, the Jewish day of Atonement. In the Old Testament, Leviticus 16 requires that two male goats and a bull be brought to the place of sacrifice. The high priest cast lots and one goat was chosen, with the bull, as a burnt offering. The second goat was the designated scapegoat. The high priest placed his hands on the head of the scapegoat and confessed the sins of the people of Israel. The goat was then led away into the wilderness, bearing the sins of the people with it; it was thrown off a precipice to be claimed by the fallen angel Azazel, thus ridding the nation of its iniquities.

National iniquities and scapegoating (ancient and modern) are further illuminated in South African novelist J. M. Coetzee's *Disgrace:*

> Scapegoating worked in practice while it still had religious power behind it. You loaded the sins of the city onto the goat's back and drove it out, and the city was cleansed. It worked because everyone knew how to read the ritual, including the gods. Then the gods died, and all of a sudden, you had to cleanse the city without divine help. Real actions were demanded instead of symbolism. The censor was born. . . . Watchfulness become the watchword: the watchfulness of all over all. Purgation was replaced by the purge. (91)

The relevance of these ideas, both for a reading *The Goat* and for a reading of contemporary American society, considerably expands the impact of Albee's play.

The title, *The Goat*, suggests other echoes from antiquity as well. At the National Archeological Museum of Naples, Italy, there is a separate gallery called the Secret Cabinet, rooms containing all the erotic art that had been found in ruins of Pompeii and Herculaneum. This gallery was locked for more than a century and a half—the entrance was, at one point, actually walled up. The Secret Cabinet was recently reopened, although the exhibition can be viewed only with a guide. The most highly prized piece of the collection is the marble sculpture called *Pan and the Goat*, a graphic depiction of the god Pan having intercourse with a goat who is lying on her back, a posture that makes it/her seem more human. The guide remarked when we arrived at this sculpture, "Look at the sweetness of her face. Look how she looks at him!" This could have been a line from Albee's play, which had not yet been written, and it was only long after that I made this startling connection.

Pan, the god of herds and flocks, was represented as a man with a goat's horns and hooves and shaggy, fur-covered legs; his sexual appetites were notoriously insatiable, and, consequently, the god could inspire overwhelming, irrational fears in men and animals. Thus the English word *panic* has his name as its root. Even more interesting for our purposes here, all wild places were his home, but

The Goat or, Who Is Sylvia? with Mercedes Ruehl and Bill Pullman, New York, 2002. (Photograph by Carole Rosegg.)

his birthplace was Arcadia, the idyllic Greek world, often used as the backdrop for pastoral poetry, evoking simplicity, peace, and quiet. Martin, while searching for a country house, is astonished by his response to the rural environment, a peaceful, Arcadian world of natural plenty, and when he tells Ross how thrilled he was, Ross cannot or will not understand. Martin tells him, "It gave me a kind of shiver," to which his friend replies, "The ludicrous often does" (3:566).

Martin tells Stevie about the moment he fell in love with Sylvia: "It was then that I saw her. And she was looking at me with . . . with those eyes. [. . .] She was looking at me with those eyes of hers and . . . I melted, I think. I think that's what I did: I melted. [. . .] I'd never seen such an expression. It was pure . . . and trusting and . . . and innocent; so . . . so guileless" (3:597). A realistic fact: unlike other barnyard animals, goats have yellow eyes with rectangular pupils, set on the side of the head; it is often hard to tell what a goat is looking at; clearly the wonder and beauty of Sylvia's gaze lies in the eyes of the beholder.

The images used to publicize productions carried their own tragicomic impact: The image used in advance of the play's world premiere, when no one knew what the play was about, showed a formal, and thus unsmiling, family portrait: seated Stevie (Mercedes Reuhl) and Martin (Bill Pullman), hands primly folded in laps, with their son Billy (Jeffrey Carlson) standing behind them, closer to mom, hand on dad's shoulder. Separating Martin and Stevie's knees is a white goat picking up the bright white of the shirt Billy (Billy the Kid? billy goat?) is wearing, while Stevie's blue blouse and Martin's blue shirt link them. The Philadelphia Theatre Company used in their advertisements a picture of a goat with a snapshot of the play's characters hanging out of its mouth, suggesting that a goat, who will, notoriously, eat anything, has devoured this family alive.

The Goat has two subtitles; the first, *Who Is Sylvia,* comes from Shakespeare's *Two Gentlemen of Verona,* where the spelling is "Silvia." *Two Gentlemen* is a troubling comedy about courtship and about friendship, about infidelity and betrayal, all the themes of Albee's play. It includes this famous song in act 4, scene 3:

Who is Silvia? What is she,
That all our swains commend her?
Holy, fair and wise is she;
The heaven such grace did lend her,
That she might admired be.

Is she kind as she is fair?
For beauty lives with kindness;
Love doth to her eyes repair,
For help him of his blindness;
And, being help'd, inhabits there.

Then to Silvia let us sing,
That Silvia is excelling;
She excels each mortal thing
Upon the dull earth dwelling;
To her let us garlands bring.

It will happen in the course of Shakespeare's play that Proteus, the second gentleman of Verona, will assail Silvia's honor; that Valentine will see and hear his treachery; and that he will finally forgive him. This is what allows the play to proceed to its comedic conclusion and the two pairs of lovers to be united at last. Forgiveness is the issue here: "were man / But constant, he were perfect: that one error / Fills him with faults; makes him run through all the sins: / Inconstancy falls off ere it begins" (5.4.110–14). Forgiveness is the redemptive act, the cornerstone of comedy. Stevie's inability or refusal to forgive creates *The Goat*'s havoc and the tragedy.

Another Shakespearean resonance worth considering is that of his "green world," a rich notion Northrop Frye put forward in his seminal work, *Anatomy of Criticism*. The "drama of the green world," as he calls it, suggests "the triumph of life and love over the wasteland" (182). It is thus a comedic mode and refers to the characters' escape into an arcadia, a magical woods where desperate lovers, mistreated children, and usurped dukes escape the tyranny of the court to find freedom in the forest, where the natural world undoes the false constraints of the "normal" world; consider *Two Gentlemen of Verona*, *Midsummer Night's Dream*, and *As You Like It*, for obvious examples. Thus the "green world" stands as the obverse of the built world.

Albee made Martin an architect; when a playwright decides on a profession for his character, it should be a meaningful choice, and Martin is not just any architect, but one of the most famous and successful architects in the world, having just won the Pritzker Prize. An architect is, necessarily, representative of the built world, a profession that, viewed from a particular angle, is necessarily antinature, since nature must, to some degree, make way for the creations of the architect-artist. Martin's stature in the architectural world requires that the play's set be remarkable; it should be a spectacularly designed house, and the objects Stevie smashes should be not only beautiful but unique—perhaps pre-Columbian pieces, or Picasso ceramics—things that once broken cannot be fixed or replaced. The wreckage of their home should mirror the wreckage of their relationship, which also cannot be fixed or replaced.

We learn that Martin is about to start his newest architectural project, the design of the "two hundred billion dollar dream city of the future, financed by U.S. Electronics Technology and set in the wheatfields of our Middle West." This project, called "The World City," is, environmentally speaking, more a nightmare than a "dream," the urbanization of the farmland of the Heartland of America, the paving over of the "green world." And if we pay attention to the mythic underpinnings of this play, underpinnings fundamental to its tragic spirit, we see that Martin's falling in love with a goat may be Mother Nature's revenge. Far beyond Oberon's merry spite in *Midsummer Night's Dream* when Bottom is turned into a donkey and Titania becomes besotted with him, this is the kind of vengeance wreaked by a scorned or neglected goddess: consider Aphrodite's revenge on Hippolytus, when, to punish him for worshiping Artemis rather than worshiping at her own altars (an obvious metaphor for his denying his sexuality) she makes his stepmother, Phaedra, fall madly in love with him, leading to a sequence of horrifying outcomes.

When Martin goes country-house-hunting, he finds himself on the "crest" of a hill, and, having bought a carful of nature's bounty, he rhapsodizes over "the roadside stands, with corn and other stuff piled high, and baskets full of other things—beans and tomatoes and those great white peaches you only get in late summer" (3:566). Although "the drama of the green world" is usually comic, here it is tragic, and even more so in that Albee sees Martin's excursion from the urban world into that fertile paradisal world as transforming but hideously nonredemptive. It is as though Albee reached into the Shakespearean sleeve and turned it inside out. Like Martin, Albee seems "deeply troubled, greatly divided" (3:603), and it is this very refusal to find a tidy moral, a point of purchase, that makes the play so interesting and so disturbing for the audience.

Stevie is reduced from the witty, civilized, interesting woman she was to a primitive creature howling with rage (the stage directions require a "huge animal sound," 3:603), thus proving Martin's point:

> STEVIE. *(After a little; teary again)* You can't fuck a soul.
> MARTIN. No; and it isn't about fucking.

STEVIE. YES!!

MARTIN. *(As gentle as possible)* No; no, Stevie, it isn't.

STEVIE. *(Pause; then, even more sure.)* Yes! It is about fucking! It is about you being an animal!

MARTIN. *(Thinks a moment; quietly)* I thought I was.

STEVIE. *(Contempt)* Hunh!

MARTIN. I thought I was; I thought we *all* were . . . animals. [. . .]

STEVIE. [. . .] You're a monster! (3:602–3)

Not only does this suggest Martin has become a monstrous creature like a Pan or a satyr, but it recalls the early, seemingly innocent but peculiarly puzzling moment near the play's start when Martin and Stevie share a laugh and he kisses her on the forehead and she says, "Oh, you know how to turn a girl on! Forehead kisses! *(Sniffs him.)* Where have you been?" (3:543). The above exchange raises again all the issues of deep division raised at the end of *The Zoo Story*, written nearly half a century earlier: the need to remain primal, animal, in order to remain fully alive, and the dangers of the alienation from self as well as from nature in becoming a fully civilized person. Consider, too, that *The Zoo Story* takes place in Central Park—a too-tame version of the green world—and recounts the story of the zoo, the antithesis of nature and animal freedom.

The play's second subtitle, *Notes Toward a Definition of Tragedy*, provides additional interpretive possibilities. The English word *tragedy* comes from the Greek word *tragidia* meaning "goat song," and one explanation of the origins of that Greek word is that the prize awarded to the best play at the festival was a goat, which was then sacrificed. Aristotle's *Poetics* provides two origins of tragedy, suggesting that it developed from the dithyramb, a choral dance performed in the worship of Dionysus; the attendants of Dionysus were also called *tragoi* because they wore goats' ears, so tragedy may have developed from the "satyric" where the *saturoi* eventually became the tragic chorus dressed as satyrs. Albee's play invites speculation about *The Goat*'s connection to the satyr plays, as well as to tragedy: Dionysus, the lord of misrule, who was also the god of theater, thus stands for theater's task to reveal a society's foolishness. Satyrs, who were forest gods, with half-human, half-goat form, manifest the basest forms of freedom through lust and drunkenness.

Bruce Fraser in his "Introduction to the Tragedies" makes this illuminating comment:

> The satyrs [the satyr plays] seem to affirm the life force at its most basic. They demand the right not always to sympathise, not to permanently share in the misery of the world, because to do so is to lose sight of what survives in the face of what is dying . . . like walking through a garden and seeing only dead leaves and ignoring the buds. Perhaps the satyr play is the necessary survival kit for compassion, a complement to tragedy, making it whole and allowing the theatre to offer not only the tragic, but also the power of recuperation, just as in real life. Greek masks of comedy and tragedy are often depicted as hanging from the same nail.

Just as tragicomedy is a twentieth-century form (Chekhov, Beckett), requiring that we weep and laugh simultaneously, so the satyr tragedy may be a newer form for our time: we laugh first and weep later, but, unlike classical tragedy, satyr tragedy eradicates catharsis, denying us what Fraser calls "recuperation." Martin is left "diminished" and Stevie has "shut [her] tragic mouth." The play's final image of bloodstained Stevie dragging in the murdered Sylvia reminds us of Orestes dragging in the murdered Clytemnestra, or Medea standing over her slaughtered children.

In ancient Greek tragedy, the hero, at the height of his happiness, often complacent in his smooth fortunate life, undergoes a sudden reversal of fortunes. This is what Stevie seems to intuit when she affectionately mocks Martin early on: "The old foreboding? The sense that everything going right is a sure sign that everything's going wrong, of all the awful to come? All that?" When, a bit later, the doorbell rings, announcing Ross's arrival, Martin quips with eerie prescience, "Ah! Doom time!" When Ross is adjusting his equipment for a voice test, he says, "I hear a kind of . . . rushing sound, like a . . . woooooosh! or wings, or something." Martin replies, "It's probably the Eumenides," but realistic Ross says, "More like the dishwasher. There; it stopped," to which Martin replies, "Then it probably wasn't the Eumenides: they don't stop" (3:551–52). The Eumenides are the domesticated, reformed Furies—the horrific harridans who hound Orestes through the world after he kills his mother, obviously an externalized manifestation of his guilt. And, given the fact that it is Martin's fiftieth birthday, that he has just won the most coveted prize in architecture, and an immense contract to build "The World City," he is, as Ross says, at the "pinnacle" of success; with appalling irony Ross exclaims that it is "probably the most important week of your life." Leaving superstitious anxieties aside, "the old foreboding" is that recognizable sense of "uh-oh" that is crucial to any dramatic plot.

The "pinnacle of his success" is a geographic metaphor for the literal "crest" of the hill on which Martin stands when he meets Sylvia—and once you are at the top, there's no place to go but down, as every tragic hero knows. Albee has shown us that "fall from a great height" which Aristotle says is a defining characteristic of tragedy.

The shock value of the central fact of the goat is so great that we try to console ourselves by thinking that bestiality is a metaphor—for homosexuality, perhaps, especially since all the characters in the play have male names. Albee denies us this easy escape; the play amply provides nonmetaphoric homosexuality in Billy. And far more shocking is the deeply moving and deeply dangerous moment in which Albee confronts us with homosexuality compounded by incest when Billy passionately kisses his father on the mouth. Albee, in Martin's voice, gives us a way to understand: it just "clicks over" (3:616), thereby comforting his son and us simultaneously. But Albee is not through shocking us; we then have to cope with Martin's story of the father holding his baby on his lap and discovering he has an erection, to which Ross reacts with, "Getting hard with a baby! Is there anything you people don't get off on!?" (3:618). Martin's response is a tirade about the extremes and vagaries of human passion (the sadomasochism of St. Sebastian's arrows, the psychosexuality of the Crucifixion) that speaks much of what Albee has been saying all along: human sexuality is more complex, far wider, deeper, and less governable than we generally think.

Ross's betrayal of Martin's confidence and of their friendship may be the most problematic of the play's many betrayals, although Ross's reasons are, if crass, realistic: "This isn't . . . embezzlement, honey; this isn't stealing from helpless widows [. . .] . This isn't the stuff that stops a career in its tracks for a little while—humiliation, public remorse, and then back up again. This is *beyond* that—*way* beyond it!" (3:620). Crass realism always betrays the tragic, and the limits of Ross's imagination cause him to be scandalized into righteous indignation and protective outrage. Ross reminds Martin that they have been friends for forty years, to which Martin replies, "Yes. That gives you something? Rights or something?" (3:556). Both the duration of their friendship and the issue of the "rights" it gives echo a nearly identical conversation in *A Delicate Balance* between Tobias and Harry.

Billy, too, is profoundly betrayed, in what may be the most fundamental betrayal, the loss of innocence: his childhood ends spectacularly as he is flung out of the paradisal happy family. He is left with no answer to his plaintive "Dad? Mom?" which ends the play.

Occupant

Albee's central character in *Occupant* is the sculptor Louise Nevelson, who was his friend for many years and who shares with her playwright a firm refusal to bend to public or critical opinion. Her refusal to snatch success by means of artistic compromise, a dominant factor of Nevelson's career, echoes Albee's own career and his adamant repudiation of pandering to commercial success, to become what he calls "an employee." By all accounts, Nevelson was, indeed, "a bird of rare plumage," as Albee calls her in his essay "Louise Nevelson," written on the occasion of the retrospective of her work at the Whitney Museum of American Art. Nevelson was a major American sculptor whose public image was as famous as her constructions, and his play *Tiny Alice* inspired one of her most famous pieces, *Mrs. N's Palace.* "She was always doing a performance. Nevelson in public was Nevelson in private," as Albee told Gussow (*ASJ,* 334).

Albee wrote *Occupant* for Anne Bancroft, but her illness prevented the production's opening in New York in 2002; the play has still not had a professional premiere. Its publication in *Collected Plays* is its first.

Appearing as in a postmortem interview, Albee's Nevelson is an artist's construction, a collaboration, it would seem, between Albee and Nevelson—part biography, part dramatic character—who emerges through and from the contentious dialogue. Man, the interviewer, is described as "40s, pleasant," albeit he seems distinctly *un*pleasant in the reading: hostile to his interviewee, obsessed with facts and details as opposed to truth and ideas. He frustrates the putative audience (frequently addressed in coy asides) by not asking the right questions; he seems insensitive to the suffering in Nevelson's life and judgmental about her weaknesses and failings. He is, in short, rude. At one point Nevelson turns to the audience and says, "He doesn't *understand* anything" (3:653). Albee's tone here is perplexing: are we supposed to like and trust Man or resent him? Is his lack of understanding Albee's version of the members of the clumsy media? Is Man a device to create sympathy for Nevelson?

Unlike most of Albee's plays, meaning in this play emerges from the visuals rather than from the language, and thus the brief clues in the stage directions are crucial. At the start, Nevelson is "encased in costume 'cage,'" expecting to be so recognizable that she needs no introduction, despite Man's attempts to present her: "You have to introduce me? People don't know who I am? They look at me up here like this *(Gestures to cage, or shell)* and they don't say 'Look, that's Louise Nevelson'?" (3:626). The "cage" is, both literally and figuratively, that construct which she both makes and takes to be her public image—no less a construction than the constructions that are her art. Thus the theatrical metaphor is extended: creating a character (consider the many meanings of the word *role* as it applies both to drama and to life) extends, in less flamboyant ways, perhaps, to anyone's identity. That it is called a "cage" signifies in obvious ways: a person, especially a public personality, is trapped in the image of the self that she has built, or that has been built for her and must, then, be inhabited. So when Man explains that with the passage of time she has grown less recognizable, he asks a question with more import than belligerence: "I mean . . . who do you think you are?" (3:627). This issue of identity is often a central one in Albee's plays, although the "Who am I?" repeated over and over in *The Lady from Dubuque* is perhaps the loudest.

The interview will rehearse the biography: Leah Berliawsky, born near Kiev in 1899, who reinvented herself through many transformations to become the "Great American Sculptor" she became. The relation between the person and the likeness—whether on stage or in sculpture—is an underlying theme of the play. This is further complicated by the relation between the internal person and the external person: "With any luck you turn into whoever you want to *be*. And with even *better* luck you turn into whoever you *should* be. No, you got somebody in you right from the start, and if you're lucky you figure out who it is and you *become* it" (3:639).

Albee is a serious collector (he prefers "accumulator") of contemporary art, and he frequently contributes to museum catalogs and curates exhibitions. For a show called "Idea to Matter," he wrote about "the fundamental difference between painting and sculpture. In painting, all is illusion: color, shape, perspective. Nothing is real beyond the illusion of reality created by the painter. It is, after all, all flat, all false, and, in the best hands, all wonderful, all real. In sculpture, everything is real: object, color, shape, perspective, and, in the best hands, all is wonderful, filled with illusion" (*SMM*, 271). In "John Duff," he writes, "Much the same as in theatre, a play is a representation of an event, while a film is a representation of a representation, a sculpture does not demand the extra artifice. Nothing pejorative is intended here, of course: all art is artifice; it is this artifice, this metaphorical distancing, which gives art its reality, its power" (*SMM*, 125). And most relevant to *Occupant* is Albee's remark about the problems of collecting sculpture: "it tends—again at its very best—to be nondecorative and intrusive (or is assertive a politer term?); very little of it tends to relate to a décor—'build around *me*!' it seems to say" (*SMM*,123). And that is exactly what we see happen, before our eyes, onstage, quite literally, in *Occupant*; perhaps this happens in any play, albeit metaphorically.

The correlation between Nevelson's process of creating her sculpture, made out of bits and pieces, found scraps retrieved from the rubbish on the streets—"broken chairs, banisters, flat pieces, anything"—and the making of an identity is what the play demonstrates before our eyes. Paralleling our accumulating knowledge about Nevelson, the stage begins to fill with wood; then a wood sculpture starts to appear, "small at first, and then bigger," and then she tells us she got the idea of "stacking up wooden boxes and putting wood inside them [. . .] it was a whole world!" (3:691). Albee translates this into stage directions: "The stage is now filled with her work" as she tells us, "All of a sudden I had become *me*, and I was *that*!" (3:692). As a playwright does, Nevelson's art created visible worlds; thus, Albee's construction, *Occupant*, contains both Nevelson and her construction. She tells Man, "But if you come *into* yourself like I did, if you finally know the space you . . . occupy. . . . well, then, you go on" (3:692).

Nevelson's own written comment on *Mrs. N's Palace* is illuminating here, especially as it could as well be a comment on the making of plays and the filling of stage space:

> I think often people don't realize the meaning of space. They think space is something empty. Actually, in the mind and the projection into this three-dimensional world, space plays the most vital part in our lives. Your concept of what you put into a space will create another space. You can see a person walk into a room and dominate the space. Space has an atmosphere, and what you put into it will color your thinking and your awareness. (161)

The occupation of space—one of the tasks of a dramatic character and one of the tasks of a work of sculpture—is significant in a play titled *Occupant*. Thus the anecdote we hear near the play's conclusion only partly explains the play's title: when she was in the hospital, dying, she had her name replaced on her room's door with "Occupant." She smiles at her explanation: "There's no privacy anywhere" (3:699). The famous—and famously constructed—self, with her signature doubled sable eyelashes, endures through photographs and Albee's homage, despite the anonymity of the sign on the last room she occupies in life. "Occupant" is a person who will cease to be, and who will, more and more frequently, need to be "introduced," as she is at the start of act 1. She necessarily reenters the carapace at play's end, and her last line, "Are we finished?" is a moving irony.

Over and over, in various contexts, Albee emphasizes that to be worthwhile, art must expand (relocate?) our judgmental boundaries, and, at the same time, be a "moral" act, in that it allows the logics and coherencies of art to affect—and effect—our responses to the world around us and its quandaries.

To the extent that we permit the arts to impinge upon our consciousness we are altered; our perceptions are either broadened or diminished. Art can enliven, and art can kill. (*SMM*, 155)

And, further, when asked about the relationship between theater and visual art, Albee replied,

All art is useful, if it's any good at all. It has to be socially useful. Anything that is merely decorative has absolutely no use at all. Anytime I go to the theatre, I feel my time has been wasted unless it has extended the boundaries of my theatrical experience and made me rethink my values. . . . Art should make some comment on how one views consciousness. It should make me think differently about consciousness and the art form itself—both. (*SMM*, 133)

Nevelson's little poem seems to be a miniature version of the play:

How long—how long
Can I sustain myself
On that littlest of platforms
Tightrope walkers
Have infinite space
      Lucky them.
    (From *Louise Nevelson*)

Knock! Knock! Who's There!?

Albee rarely forgoes an opportunity to make a snide remark about reviewers; like many playwrights, but more than most authors of his stature, his relationship with critics has always been vexed: defensive, disparaging of their intelligence, their analytical abilities, and their capacity for fairness, he often represents them as an antiart brigade. This hostility reaches its comic peak in his tiny play *Knock! Knock! Who's There!?* in which he imagines a critic trapped and calling for help from behind a door. The door is not only locked, but someone has hastily nailed boards across it, and Albee's prefatory directions suggest this spot be located in some semiremote part of the theater that audience members are likely to pass—a corridor on the way to the restrooms, for example. The sounds—both the voice and the pounding—are recorded, although I suspect Albee would prefer the performance to be live; one imagines it would be easy to find an actor to perform the voice who would also relish this oblique revenge. Exceeding—or perhaps undermining or perhaps fulfilling—Albee's revenge fantasy, in the premiere performance at McCarter Theatre, Bruce Weber, theater critic for the *New York Times*, played the voice, shouting his lines, "Help!" and "Hello?" and "I'm a critic! Let me out!" (3:704).

There is a history of playwrights' revenge plays; the funniest of them may be Tom Stoppard's *The Real Inspector Hound*, in which two critics, sitting in the audience waiting for the play to begin, eventually become involved in the murder mystery onstage. It is both hilarious and profound, commenting on dramatic illusion—the relation between play and audience, character and actor, and all the other permutations and combinations of the theatrical enterprise—while also achieving an ornate revenge. As one character says near the end, as he fatally shoots the critic, "I have waited a long time for this moment." Samuel Beckett did not need to write a whole play to achieve his revenge, but managed with just one word in *Waiting for Godot*. Vladimir and Estragon are trading insults as an amusement to pass the time. They begin their verbal attacks with "Moron!" and "Vermin!" and escalate the venom through "Cretin!" Estragon ends the exchange with the unanswerable worst: "Crritic!" Vladimir "wilts, vanquished."

Anyone who has attended the Humana Festival in Louisville, Kentucky, a venue noted for introducing new American plays, knows that there are, in addition to a long roster of productions, various clever nonstage performances; these extras have included, for instance, phone banks where you pick up a receiver and hear a two-minute play through the receiver; those scripts are always about phone calls. Another unconventional approach are T-shirts imprinted with short plays on the back, written for the occasion by famous playwrights (Tony Kushner, David Henry Hwang, etc.); these plays' plots always turn on T-shirts. During the annual Festival there is a "Critic's Weekend" where all the plays in the festival's schedule—as many as fourteen—are squashed into one long weekend, allowing hundreds of critics from all over the country and the world to see all the shows. *Knock! Knock! Who's There!?* would be hilariously perfect for this venue, since the audience is made up entirely of critics.

Despite Albee's having concluded with a *jeu d'esprit*, the three-volume collection stands as testimony to the immense contribution he has made to the canon of dramatic literature, while all their many productions testify to his immense contribution to the world's theater. In a recent newspaper interview, Albee told the reporter, just a few weeks before his seventy-ninth birthday, "I don't think I've written my best play yet" ("Life Must Have a Little Drama"). Albee's introduction to volume 3, written in 2005, ends with his hopes for another volume. With two as yet unpublished new plays—"Homelife" and "Me, Myself and I"—volume 4 seems well on its way.

Bibliography

Albee, Edward. "Borrowed Time: An Interview with Edward Albee." Interview by Stephen Bottoms. *The Cambridge Companion to Edward Albee*, ed. Bottoms. Cambridge: Cambridge University Press, 2005.

Albee, Edward. *The Collected Plays of Edward Albee*. 3 vols. Woodstock, NY: Overlook Duckworth, 2004–5.

Albee, Edward. "Easter Island: The Dream at the End of the World." *New York Times*, April 30, 2006, Section 5, pp. 1, 8, 9.

Albee, Edward. "Homelife (A play in one scene)." Typescript, version 1.

Albee, Edward. Interview by Charlie Rose. *The Charlie Rose Show*, PBS, May 31, 2002.

Albee, Edward. *Stretching My Mind*. New York: Caroll and Graf, 2005.

Albee, Edward. *Who's Afraid of Virginia Woolf?* New York: Signet, 1962.

Albee, Edward. "Yes Is Better Than No." Interview by Steven Samuels. *American Theatre* 11, no. 7 (1994): 38.

Albertson, Chris. *Bessie*. New York: Stein and Day, 1972.

Beckett, Samuel. *That Time*. In *Collected Shorter Plays*. New York: Grove Press, 1984.

Bigsby, C. W. E. *A Critical Introduction to Twentieth-Century American Drama*. Vol. 2. Cambridge: Cambridge University Press, 1984.

Brook, Peter. *The Empty Space*. New York: Atheneum, 1968.

Caldwell, Christopher. "Who Invented Lolita?" *New York Times Magazine*, May 23, 2004.

Coetzee, J. M. *Disgrace*. New York: Penguin, 2000.

Davis, Angela Y. *Blues Legacies and Black Feminism: Gertrude "Ma" Rainey, Bessie Smith, and Billie Holiday*. New York: Pantheon, 1998.

Edemariam, Aida. "Whistling in the Dark." *The Guardian*, January 10, 2004. http://arts.guardian.co.uk/features/ story/0,11710,1119811,00 .html, consulted June 1, 2007.

"Edward Albee." http://www.doollee.com/PlaywrightsA/albee-edward.html, consulted June 1, 2007.

Esslin, Martin. "'Dead! And Never Called Me Mother!': The Missing Dimension in American Drama." *Public Issues, Private Tensions: Contemporary American Drama*. Ed. Matthew C. Roudane. New York: AMS Press, 1993.

Esslin, Martin. *The Theatre of the Absurd*. 3rd ed. New York: Penguin, 1983.

Fraser, Bruce. "Introduction to the Tragedies." Cambridge Classics. http://www.cus.cam.ac.uk~blf10/trapedyhtml#list.

Frye, Northrop. *Anatomy of Criticism: Four Essays.* New York: Atheneum, 1966.

Gussow, Mel. *Edward Albee: A Singular Journey.* New York: Applause, 2001.

Hazlitt, William Carew 's *English Proverbs and Proverbial Phrases Collected from the Most Authentic Sources.* London: Reeves and Turner, 1907.

Isherwood, Christopher. "All Over." *Variety*, February 19, 2002. http://www.variety.com/review/VE1117917044.html?categoryid=33&cs=1, consulted May 31, 2007.

Jarvis, Gail. "Remembering Bessie Smith." http://www.lewrockwell.com/orig/jarvis6.html, consulted June 6, 2007.

Lahr, John. "Sons and Mothers." *The New Yorker*, May 16, 1994, 102–5.

Lawson, Mark. "But Where's His Mobile?" *The Guardian*, February 1, 2007.

"Life Must Have a Little Drama." *South Florida Sun Sentinal*, February 25, 2007.

Louise Nevelson. Museum of Fine Arts of Houston, October 23–December 14, 1969.

Miller, Arthur. *All My Sons.* Ed. C. W. E. Bigsby. New York: Dramatists Play Service, 1999.

Miller, Arthur. *The Last Yankee: With a New Essay about Theatre Language.* New York: Penguin, 1994.

Nevelson, Louise. *Louise Nevelson: Atmospheres and Environments.* New York: Clarkson N. Potter, in association with the Whitney Museum of American Art, 1980.

Nightingale, Benedict. "Stage View: There Really Is a World beyond 'Diaper Drama.'" *New York Times*, January 1, 1984.

Rich, Frank. "Stage: Drama by Albee, 'Man Who Had 3 Arms.'" *New York Times*, April 6, 1983.

Stewart, Patrick. "Beam Me Up, Patrick Stewart." Interview by Toby Zinman. *American Theatre*, 15, no. 2 (1998): 12–15, 68–70.

Wallenberg, Christopher. "Big Bad *Woolf.*" *Playbill*, March 11, 2005, pp. 10, 12.

Zinoman, Jason. "On Stage and Off." *New York Times*, April 2, 2004, Section E, Column 3, 2.

Chronology of Plays

This list omits those plays (*Fam and Yam*, 1959, and *The Lorca Play*, 1992) that were omitted by Edward Albee from his *Collected Plays*.

The Zoo Story (1958)
Premiere: Berlin, 1959. American premiere, New York City, 1960.

The Death of Bessie Smith (1959)
Premiere: Berlin, 1960. American premiere, New York City, 1961, directed by Alan Schneider.

The Sandbox (l959)
Premiere: New York City, 1960.

The American Dream (1960)
Premiere: New York City, 1961, directed by Alan Schneider.

Who's Afraid of Virginia Woolf? (1962)
Premiere: New York City, directed by Alan Schneider, starring Uta Hagen and Arthur Hill.
Film version released 1966, directed by Mike Nichols, starring Elizabeth Taylor and Richard Burton.

The Ballad of the Sad Café (1963)
Adapted from the novel by Carson McCullers. Premiere: New York City, directed by Alan Schneider, starring Colleen Dewhurst.

Tiny Alice (1964)
Premiere: New York City, directed by Alan Schneider, starring John Geilgud and Irene Worth.

Malcolm (1966)
Adapted from the novel by James Purdy. Premiere: New York City, 1966, directed by Alan Schneider, with Estelle Parsons.

A Delicate Balance (1966, Pulitzer Prize)
Premiere: New York City, directed by Alan Schneider, starring Jessica Tandy, Hume Cronyn.
Film version released 1973, directed by Tony Richardson, starring Katherine Hepburn and Paul Scofield.

Everything in the Garden (1967)
Adaptation from the play by Giles Cooper. Premiere: New York City, directed by Peter Glenville.

Box and *Quotations from Chairman Mao Tse-Tung* (1968)
Premiere: Buffalo, NY, directed by Alan Schneider

All Over (1971)
Premiere: New York City, directed by John Geilgud, starring Jessica Tandy and Colleen Dewhurst.

Seascape (1975, Pulitzer Prize)
Premiere: New York City, directed by Edward Albee, starring Deborah Kerr, Barry Nelson, Frank Langella, and Maureen Anderman.

Listening (1976)
Radio premiere on BBC 3, codirected by John Tydeman and Edward Albee, starring Irene Worth.
Stage premiere: 1977, Hartford, CT, directed by Edward Albee, starring Angela Lansbury.

Counting the Ways (1977)
Premiere: Hartford, CT, directed by Edward Albee, starring Angela Lansbury and William Prince.

The Lady from Dubuque (1980)
Premiere: New York City, directed by Alan Schneider, starring Irene Worth.

Lolita (1981)
Adapted from the novel by Vladimir Nabokov. Premiere: New York City, directed by Frank Dunlop, starring Donald Sutherland.

The Man Who Had Three Arms (1983)
Premiere: New York City, directed by Edward Albee, starring Robert Drivas.

Finding the Sun (1983)
Premiere: University of Northern Colorado, Greeley, directed by
Edward Albee.

Marriage Play (1987)
Premiere: Vienna, directed by Edward Albee.
American premiere: 1992, Houston, directed by Edward Albee, starring
Shirley Knight and Tom Klunis.

Three Tall Women (1991, Pulitzer Prize)
Premiere: Vienna, directed by Edward Albee, starring Myra Carter.
American premiere: 1992,Woodstock, NY, directed by Lawrence Sacharow.

Fragments (1993)
Premiere: Cincinnati, directed by Edward Albee.

The Play About the Baby (1998)
Premiere: London, directed by Howard Davies.
American premiere: 2000, Houston, directed by Edward Albee.

The Goat or, Who Is Sylvia? (2002)
Premiere: New York City, directed by David Esbjornson, starring Mercedes
Ruehl, Bill Pullman, Stephen Rowe, and Jeffrey Carlson.

Occupant (2002)
Preview performances, directed by Anthony Page, starring Anne Bancroft
and Neal Huff; due to illness, the play never officially opened.

Knock! Knock! Who's There!! (2003)
Premiere: Princeton, NJ, starring Bruce Weber.

Peter and Jerry (act 1, "Homelife," act 2, *The Zoo Story*) (2004)
Premiere: Hartford, CT, starring Johanna Day, Frank Wood, and Frederick
Weller.